To MilaMovie

May all your dreams
Come true. and May.
you have lots of love

every day.

1

Forward

The early sun glinted upon the snow and spread out a blanket of pink before me. The blanket of snow sparkled in the sunrise light and I took it in with a deep shivery breath – admiring God's morning art. It was early…and it was bitter cold and a little windy, but I didn't mind. I was on my way to pick up eight puppies that had been abandoned at the roadside - left for dead to either starve or freeze to death. It was bad enough that someone would do this to any living thing, but to do this to little innocent puppies is almost unthinkable. But unfortunately, the world is not always kind and in the rescue business we often see the unthinkable. So I focused on my mission – and enjoyed the beauty of the day break on my way.

When I got to the home of the kind woman had found the puppies, I looked into a small wooden box filled with blankets to find eight shivering black and white spotted babies….clinging to each other to get warm. "Take them just as they are…" She said "Keep the blankets! Poor babies! Thank you so much for coming!" I could tell she was as upset as I was at the person who might have done this. As I pushed my face deeper into their little wooden-box world – I tried to breathe on all of them to make them warmer. "Do you want to come home with me?" I said to them…which made me stop and smile about what I had just said.

How often I have heard other people ask that same question of a dog they have just met…a prospective adoptee to a future family member – as if permission must be granted by the dog. How sweet that the people ask the question…often while the dog is licking their faces or hugging them over their shoulder. – As if the dog would say no! Dogs – I have found – know only unconditional love. They love everyone and see them as way better than they are. They are forgiving and they seem to have sense about humanity that we all have yet to learn… Which is maybe why – as humans we feel we must ask the question.

Fortunately – I have never met a Rescue dog that would say no to going to a place where they will be loved and cared for. A warm place, a happy place that is better than anything they have ever known… This is the dream of every Rescue dog. It is the dream of every living being….This is the dream…

As I placed the wooden box with the still shivering puppies on the floor of my jeep and headed back to the rescue with full heat blasting on their little wooden box, I smiled again at God's handiwork of the day. Now full sun hit the snow and little rainbow sparkles lined my path. I looked at the pups again and was instantly reminded of why I do rescue work. I was brought to prayer of thanksgiving – for my little passengers and for my own life made so meaningful by the One who had once rescued me.

"God, Thank you for these Puppies….Thank you for this beautiful morning that I can go about doing some of your work for them - and giving back just a fraction of all you do for me. As I have rescued them – I know full well the many ways you have rescued me … And I promise to look to you and point to you with all that I do - until my work here is done. And I can only hope that you find me worthy….and when that time comes you will smile and ask 'Do you want to come home with me?'"

"A Lid for Every Pot"

Mikey and his sister Molly were both Beagle and Cocker Spaniel Mixes….about 1 year old and very nice dogs….They were both very well trained & housebroken - which is a huge plus for a rescue dog without a pedigree. As a "Mutt" – dogs are at the mercy of their own genetics – and Mickey and Molly – though full siblings – were about as different as night and day in looks…..Molly had gotten the best of both breeds in her bloodline….She had the build of a beagle and the fur of a Cocker Spaniel….She had long beautiful ears and gorgeous big round and soft eyes….Molly got a home right away. She was female – which most people want anyway – and she, of course – was beautiful….

Mickey, was a little nothing of a dog. He had obviously gotten his looks from the back waters of the gene-pool…He was skinny - with airplane ears...and a weird looking nose….He was awkward. But what he lacked in looks – he definitely made up for in manners. Mickey was SUCH a good dog!! He was so smart & he listened so well. His main goal in life was to please his master….and as his "Foster Master" I fell in love with his amazing personality and his playful nature.

Often people would ask about him from the website. In fact, he went on lots of meet & greets - but Mickey always ended up riding back home with me after watching his rescue mates get adopted. He was passed over - time after time. I would tell him on those rides home that it just wasn't his time yet - but told him that someday it would be his turn. Mickey was with us for a long time – and I often got tired of people looking at him momentarily and then going for the smaller, cuter, fluffier dogs that could never match Mickey in discipline or ability to learn and please. But I knew that it would be for him like it was for most of us in life....If we wait on the right people to love us for who we are – then we will be certain that we are with the one that God intended just for us!!

Enter Jeff & his wife Christie, a couple from Brimfield. Jeff called me & told me his co-worker had gotten her Lab mix from me & that it had been such a great fit. She had recommended he call me to get a family dog. He asked me what I had and I hesitantly began telling him about Mickey. "He's a good dog," I said "A little spaniel - a little beagle...nothing special..." I warned him, "But he is housebroken and so smart." "I was thinking of a beagle" Jeff said "We'd really like to meet him." As it turned out, I had to transport a dog to a nearby town the same morning I got the call from Jeff - so Jeff & Christie agreed to meet me...and Mickey.

I tried to be low key and not get too excited for Mickey - but I really was very hopeful. On the way up I prayed to God that this would be the day, and as Mickey rode in the front seat with me, I stroked his head – anticipating that this may be his last trip...his last disappointment.

As he emerged from the car, Jeff & Christie dropped to the ground while Mickey immediately wiggled & wriggled over to them. He licked their faces. He sat at their feet and he did great on the leash. They were taking their time with him - & I kept looking at them, praying....& listening. Where most people had - at this point patted his head and shrugged - saying "He's really not what we're looking for..." Jeff and Christie were saying "He's a good looking dog!!" Before I could whisper another prayer, Jeff was lifting Mickey onto his shoulder and saying "Do you want to come home with me?"

Joy surged through my heart and tears came involuntarily into my eyes....I literally heard myself say "Oh – Thank God!" out loud!!!

"We think he's perfect!"......Said Jeff – and they quickly signed the agreement and paid the adoption fee for Mickey....

My mother always says "There is a lid for every pot"...and though I don't like to think of my little angels or their people as lids or pots - it is an appropriate analogy when observing how my Mickey finally found the right fit with a family that would love him for who he was. As I handed the adoption agreement to the beaming couple from Brimfield, I bent down to Mickey and kissed his nose. Between genuine kisses from his little tongue and my own happy tears I whispered to him "It's your turn, buddy. It's your turn." And I knew he finally understood what I had promised him all along. It did happen for him, some day. And today was that day!!

"For I know the plans I have for you," says the Lord. "They are plans for good and not for disaster, to give you a future and a hope." Isaiah 29:11-12:

"For Pete's Sake!"

When Beau & Sue lost their beloved Mr. Bill - they felt a loss like most pet owners do when they have to let go of a precious furry loved one. They put away Mr. Bill's special items, talked about their cherished memories of their 11 year old fox terrier, and waited until their hearts healed enough to accept a new "Baby" into their lives. When they had finally decided it was time to go ahead and get another little one to fill that void - they let their family know that they were indeed looking...and decided to wait to find just the right puppy. As God would have it - they would not have to wait very long.

I have found so many times in this line of work that there are just no coincidences. God always has a plan on exactly where to place each of his very special doggies - and I would certainly say that this was the case with Sue and Beau. Just Monday - her daughter in law, Peggy contacted me to see if I had any little ones ready for adoption. I did not.....But just a half an hour later - I got a message from the Pound - telling me about three puppies that were coming in who needed rescued. Unfortunately - I could not get to them until Wednesday, and by the time I got there at 7 in the morning only one was left. The others had been adopted - which is a very good thing in the realm of rescue. The last one would have probably gotten adopted, too - but there he sat in a huge cell crying and crying - all by himself. I had to take him because he looked so lonely.

When I got home - I posted his picture on Facebook as I always do – and for some reason – I called him "Pete". I then sent the picture to Peggy. She immediately sent it to Sue and they called me and said they wanted to see the puppy that afternoon.

8

Within an hour - I was at Sue and Beau's house in Magnolia with the puppy. Peggy and her daughters were there, too. We watched him run around and Sue started calling him "Pete". I looked at Peggy and asked her if she had told her the name I had posted for him on Facebook. "No" Peggy replied "When she saw his picture - she said 'Aww he looks like a Pete!'" That, I thought, was a good sign. As I said - there are just no coincidences in this business!! But I was still apprehensive. Pete had some big shoes to fill. Mr.Bill was obviously a big part of their lives and they missed him terribly.

Sue was immediately smitten. Pete was already following her around and climbing up her legs to get kisses....Beau was another story. He was a bit aloof. He did not interact with the pup right away. He was concerned with the training of the pup and the overall health of the pup - as any good prospective owner might be. He watched the pup...he pet the pup. But he didn't interact with the pup right away. Sue kept looking at him sideways and saying "What do you think?" She was already a goner!! She was in love....But Beau was cautious. "He's Nice...He's Good", he would say. Finally Sue said out loud what the rest of us were thinking. "He is not Mr. Bill....No dog will be Mr. Bill. But he is a sweet baby..." Then their granddaughter Isabelle piped up and said "He is not Mr. Bill, Grandpa - He is Mr. Pete!"

Whatever magical incantation those words held - they seemed to work on Beau. Maybe it was simplicity of the youngest person of the room stating the obvious - or maybe it was that special love that a Grandpa has for his Granddaughters that touched him and literally moved him from his seat....but in a few seconds - Beau was down on the floor with Pete. He was laying down and letting Pete come to him. Pete was jumping all over him and Beau was letting him - allowing the bond to form and grow. In a few minutes Beau was smiling at Pete - and talking to him....He even took Pete outside for his first 'Planned' Pottie break.

Inside my heart - I said a silent prayer of thanks - knowing that Pete had found a home - and the healing for Sue and Beau could begin. Isabelle had said it all....They could not replace Mr. Bill - but here was Mr. Pete - needing them just as much as they needed him. God knew it way before any of us...and He made it all happen so that what was lost could be found....and what was missing could be filled again - with warm wet kisses and cold nose nudges to grow a new and lasting love.
Or to put it more succinctly - For Pete's sake - there are just no coincidences!!!

"Remember not the former things, nor consider the things of old. Behold, I am doing a new thing; now it springs forth, do you not perceive it? I will make a way in the wilderness and rivers in the desert." Isaiah 43: 18-19

"Waiting on God's Time"

"All in God's time"....That is what I always say. But it seemed like NO time was going to be Spike's lucky day. Poor Spike was dumped off at the home of my bank manager Cari's house in June. He had been with us most of the summer and had been advertised, shown, and ultimately rejected by prospective adopters a good number of times. To some degree - I understood. Spike was not exactly an easy sell. He had some strikes against him. He was part Jack Russell - not everyone likes a Jack Russell....not everyone likes having dogs that are smarter than they are....He was medium sized and a terrier....not the cute and fuzzy little type of dog that most people want. But Spike was a really good dog. He was always smiling. Always ready for fun. He was great on a leash and could learn just about any trick in a very short time. Still, he was here longer than most dogs who come into rescue....His outlook seemed grim....but I was prepared to keep feeding him and loving him until he found a home - however long that took.

Well - yesterday was Spike's Lucky Day!! I had advertised Spike yet again on the rescue website and in the paper - hoping this would be the weekend for him. The weekend passed.....without any interest.... But yesterday - A fella named Jim called me and asked "About the white terrier"....I nearly fainted!!! I told him all about Spike and how he came to be with us.

He told me he had gotten a dog about a year ago from the Trumbull County pound that had also been dumped...."All he had when they found him was a note attached to his collar that looked like it was written by an old person. It said 'My name is Brecken.' He is all white and has just a little brown on his ear and a brown patch on his eye"

11

He said "Brecken looks just like Spike! That is why I had to call!!"
I made plans to meet him and hopefully Spike would get a home. I was
getting excited. How awesome that Spike would have a friend to play with
and a new family to call his OWN!!! When the man and his wife rolled up
in the truck - they got out and immediately fell in love with Spike. He
jumped up carefully and gave them both kisses as they kneeled beside him
- and Spike included me in the kissing fest.

I said to Jim - who was already putting a nice leather collar he had bought
around Spike's neck "I cannot believe we had him this long....He is just
the best!" Jim nodded - "Brecken is so smart and such a good boy - I know
some people don't go for the terriers - but I wouldn't have another kind of
dog" He said "I just know that they will have a blast together."

Jim and his wife Melanie put Spike in the front seat with them and waved
as they drove away with good old Spike!!
Later that night - about 7pm my phone started going crazy. I picked it up
and looked at it and saw I had several picture messages. My phone is not
the best in picture quality but once all of the pictures were Uploaded - I
got teary eyed once I realized what I was looking at.....Two white dogs -
walking along a fence with a swimming pool beside a pretty brick house
somewhere out in the country. Spike and Brecken were literally walking
together in these pictures – with their noses together. It was as if they had
been waiting all this time - to finally find each other....and be best
friends.....All in God's time!!!

"Wait for the Lord; be strong, and let your heart take courage; wait for
the Lord!" Psalm 27:14

"Surprise!"

I agreed to follow Monnie - a sweet 73-year old lady - home - so that her husband could pick out his 75th surprise birthday gift – One of three yorkie-poo puppies that Monnie had arranged for me to bring for this surprise. We met just down the road from their home and she explained to me that she had tried just about everything to get her husband to go out and get another dog – but he wouldn't hear of it…."He is still mourning the loss of our dog and he is afraid to get that wrapped up in a dog again. But if Mohammed won't go to the mountain – then I think I have to bring the mountain to Mohammed – so to speak…." She said ….Her husband had no idea we were coming - and she said he kept saying that he didn't want a dog. "But he's been lost since our dog died. You just follow my lead."

She first went in the house & said "Harry - I hit this lady's car…to which I heard Harry exclaim -"Son-of-a …!" Then she soothed it over telling him I was actually a rescue lady - & I was here with puppies. He sat back in his chair and put his hands defiantly on his knees and peered at me with a slightly perturbed but knowing grin.

"I'm sorry I lied to you - but isn't that better than a car accident?" she asked him - giggling….

He started laughing as I pulled 3 three cute little black yorkie-poos out of the carrier. The pups crawled around the floor - while he told me stories of their dog Newton - who had just died three months ago. I watched as Monnie played with the pups - holding them up for Harry to see. Pretty quickly - one of them kept going back & forth between them - paying much more attention to either of them than the other two puppies who were still crawling all over the place... Harry kept on telling his stories - while Monnie settled on playing with the pup that had obviously chosen THEM.

Finally - Monnie said "Harry, you have to concentrate on these pups. Don't you want one?" she asked - putting the pup in Harry's lap - at which point it rolled over on its back - looked up at Harry, and - as if on cue said..."Yelp!"

Harry's mouth became puckery & his eyes got twinkly & moist..& he looked at Monnie with the most loving look. "Of course I do." Harry said. Monnie got teary-eyed, too.

"Well - which one Harry?" she said looking down at the pup in his arms. He laughed & cried - all at the same time & said "Well the one that picked you out seems to be fine with me!" They hadn't even noticed I put the other two pups back in the carrier quite a while before that. That pup was supposed to be their new baby. The pup knew it before Harry did - but I have a feeling that Harry is pretty easy to train. Happy 75th Birthday Harry....Monnie, the pup and I all love you!!

"Surprise us with love at daybreak; then we'll skip and dance all the day long." Psalm 90:14

"Comfort and Joy, Comfort and Joy."

I got a call from an older man named John who was interested in Oscar - one of two Cairn Terrier mixes that came to the rescue from a high-kill shelter in Southern Ohio. When John called – he talked at length about his little terrier that had passed away just a few months ago. His voice was thick with grief – and the more he talked about the dog he lost – the more I was worried about his choice in the little one he had picked out….This dog was shy and afraid – the little fella had never really had a chance to bond with people because he had been in a kennel for a very long time…..

"I even have trouble getting him in and out of his cage because he is so shy…" I warned him…But John was pretty certain that he was very interested in this little dog. I tried very hard to bring him some comfort over the loss of his doggie – and at the same time warn him he may not be able to bond with this shy little doggie.

"Well," John Said "he looks harmless enough," - He said "Bring him along so I can see what he's like."

I agreed to meet him so that he could see the Cairn Mix doggie….As it happened I was meeting other people at the same place with a boisterous litter of beagle pups….Everyone was waiting for me as I pulled into the parking lot 40 miles from the rescue. I was so hopeful that lots of doggies could get homes that day!!

People clamored around the van as soon as I parked – and I felt I needed to wait on everyone at once….but I was concerned about John and looked around frantically for him….Fortunately, John was easy to spot – He had a big old pick-up truck and he walked slowly over to the van. He was dressed in blue jeans and a plain white T-shirt…all dressed up to meet me and Oscar. I lifted Oscar out of the van and put him in his arms "Go ahead & talk to the other families" he said "I want to talk to Oscar." And while I did - he got down on the ground – and spoke very softly to Oscar. I busied myself with the business of getting lots of puppies homes and when I completed the last interview and transaction – I turned around to see Oscar in John's lap - resting his head on John's round belly. The old guy had tears in his eyes and tears running off his chin onto his Plain white T-shirt.

John held out some money and he wiped his face. "I want him. I definitely want him." He said…His voice still thick – but this time with Joy….

Oh - by the way - John looked just like Santa Clause. And I don't think that John, Oscar, or I could have been any happier at that moment.

"Fear not, for I have redeemed you; I have called *you* by your name; You *are* Mine." Isaiah 43

"The Maltese Blessing"

When Tammy's house burned down on January 1 of this year....her beloved dachshund was the only living thing that did not make it out. "All six of us got out....except my dog, Tink." She said...."I stood there calling her name 'Tink! Tink!' but she died in there." I met Tammy at the Walmart parking lot in Massillon. She had seen one of my postings and called me about the Maltese dogs I had rescued. She lived in Applecreek - right down the road from where her house had burned down and her dog had perished.....and she was finally ready to adopt another doggie.

I really did not know Tammy's story when I agreed to meet her. Just knew she said she had wanted to adopt a Maltese. She said every Maltese she found was adorable – but so expensive. She called me and asked about Micki when she saw my little ad in the paper for her...I had talked to lots of people about Micki – but there was something in Tammy's voice that made me decide to meet her and I was so glad that I did....When I met her - she just had this demeanor of urgency about her. As we pulled into our meeting place - she ran out of her door, came around her minivan, and scooped up little Micki into her arms.......Funny thing was - Micki the Maltese - who is usually extremely shy - flew into her arms and immediately started giving her kisses - on her chin and her face.....I stood there dumbfounded as she poured out her story......

She said through her tears "I have been waiting on this one..." She said of Micki..."I tried to get a Maltese back in April....from a lady that wanted quite a bit of money for one - and my husband was going to get it for me.....but I just wasn't ready...It wasn't time," she said....."Tink meant the

17

world to me. And she would lay in my arms - just like this one is doing now." And the whole time that Tammy spoke about her pain and the tragedy of her family's loss - Micki kept kissing her face. At one point he even gave her kisses on her lips - causing her to pause and both of us to just burst into giggles.

Then she said something that gave me chills "This is so weird...." Tammy said...."New Year's Eve my whole family came up to our church for a New Year's Eve party.....We all went forward and got saved....my whole family and my cousins and relatives from out of town. 3:00 am the next morning my house burned down. You would think that would turn a person against God, wouldn't you?" She smiled "But instead He has just been Blessing us ever since....In all kinds of ways." She said "It was like our old lives were consumed by that fire - and we were given a new life when we all got saved.....It was like we were re-born through that Fire.....except for losing Tink.....Now getting Micki.....This just makes it complete."

We stood in the parking lot - knowing it was time to part - but we were having "Church" - and neither of us wanted to leave that divine appointment that was brought about by my little ad - but most obviously coordinated by the Omnipotence of Our Savior. I think I hugged her about six or seven times before our final goodbye. Micki was still busy kissing her - so I just kissed the top of his head and told him "You are right where you belong, buddy!" I drove off - watching him still kissing her and her talking to him, no doubt telling him all about Tink - and thanking God for His guidance in giving them both a new life!

"Therefore if anyone is in Christ, he is a new creature; the old things passed away; behold, new things have come. " 2 Corinthians 5:17

"Blinner"

Blinner - at least we think that was his name - came to us early in the summer from a family who was deaf. The mother and daughter were heartbroken that they had to give him up....Unfortunately - their deafness prevented them from hearing the dog barking when he was tied outside - they had accumulated several citations. They had no choice but to find him a new home or allow the city to take him to the pound.

When his owner brought him, of course there was somewhat of a language barrier....She was deaf and spoke sign language - but I had learned enough signing from some deaf friends of mine - and knew the sign language alphabet enough to reassure her that Blinner - at least we think was his name - would be in good hands and would find a home. I let her have as much time saying goodbye to him as she wanted and when she signed to me that she was ready - we took Blinner in, I hugged her, and Blinner was a full-fledged resident of the shelter.

The reason we never knew Blinner's name - was because his people always spelled his name out on paper or in texts as. "Bliner" or "Dliner" - and since neither of the former owners could speak - we were not sure if this was a signing notation - or if that is just what they called him between each other in sign language. The dog - at first- did not respond to spoken language and he was almost impossible to catch when he was in the back yard.....We figured if he knew anything at all of a spoken language - it would be a high-pitched inflection that people who cannot hear themselves talk often use....As politically incorrect as it may seem - we tried that on the dog. The first time we did it - he jumped - stopped and sat perfectly still.....He began to sit and give his paw to us when commanded with this inflection. It was a break through - and we were then able to make him see that we were to be trusted and he began to learn commands and speech as a part of his new life. We began calling him "Blinner - and it stuck ... Blinner was with us for a long time. Often passed over for pups or little dogs - his somewhat large frame needed a special household that could take his size. He was a mellow and sweet dog...and somewhat shy.....And mostly - homeless - for a very long time. Blinner really needed a home! Thankfully, Rhondalynn called us last weekend. She had seen Blinner on the website and fallen in love with his coloring and his sweet face. She said she had been looking a long time for a dog that was somewhat mature and would fit her household and give her children and grandchildren love. We assured her that Blinner was full of love - for everyone.

We agreed to meet on a Monday evening - and we drove up to Akron - hopeful that there would be a good connection between Blinner and Rhondalynn....But we didn't need to worry....Because when Blinner met Rhondalynn - he jumped - literally - into her arms and figuratively - at the chance to have a new life with a new family that he could love.

After we had signed the agreements and all of our paper work was done - Rhondalynn stood petting Blinner's head and asked us "Now what is his name? Why is his name Blinner?" We told her the story of where Blinner had come from and how we were never really sure what his name was." And she kneeled down to Blinner and said "What a hard thing for a dog - to not hear your name..." Blinner smiled his big dog smile and kissed her face. "Come on Blinner, let's go home!!"

Again Blinner jumped - this time into her car - and again - at the chance of having a new life.

As they drove away - Blinner sat up in the back seat - and looked around out of the windows. He looked so happy to be going home to a place where he would be spoiled and he could spoil his family back with love. Knowing that Blinner is finally so happy - made us want to jump...for joy!

"Rejoice in that day and leap for joy, because great is your reward in heaven. " Luke 6:23

"Second Chance, Buster!"

Buster came to us from an Amish farm in the Spring of 2012…He was four or five years old – and had been used as a Yorkshire Terrier stud in a puppy mill.…To say that Buster was frightened when he got to the shelter was a bit of an understatement.…Buster was terrified. I could not so much as touch the top of his head without sending him into a barking fit and causing him to try to attack my hands and arms with his tiny sharp little teeth…I was very much afraid that I might have to put Buster down because he was vicious.

But – one day I was snacking on a chocolate chip cookie in front of Buster outside in the backyard – and dropped part of it on the ground. He lunged forward before I could even try to pick up the cookie and he ate it all up so quickly – I wondered how a little dog like that would have managed crunching up the cookie that fast! After that day – I began taking a half of a cookie to him at various times of the day. He was always so happy to see the cookie – and eventually – while he was snacking and smacking his lips – I was touching him lightly on the head. Eventually, he allowed me access to his kennel and then he allowed me to touch him – without the use of a cookie.

As summer stretched out and the days and weeks were measured by cookies in front of Buster's kennel…I gained that little boy's trust. I looked at it as a personal challenge – I was faced with the do or die opportunity to change this little guy's life and I was not going to give up! Even if it took me all summer – I was going to make sure he knew that he was worthy of love and could truly be transformed from a scared little kennel dog to a dog of distinction!

Finally – after weeks of working with him, and taking him for rides in the car – and carrying him around and teaching him his name - I realized he was probably ready for a home. And just a few days after I pronounced him "adoptable" - a couple actually called me and asked me if I had a Yorkie. I told them "Well, I have a Yorkie - he is an Amish rescue and still needs some training – but he is a great little guy!" They said they wanted to meet him....!!

I had a really good feeling about them right away – and I was thrilled when this middle-aged couple gravitated immediately towards Buster. And Buster was absolutely charming - winding himself around them and doing great on the leash and collar I had been working with on him. He jumped up to greet them and was just adorable!! I told them about his history and about how he would not let me touch him when he first came to me....I told him how I won him over with chocolate chip cookies and how he had become just a very happy and sweet boy who loved everyone.

And while I went on with Buster's story - the lady who was cuddling Buster in her arms began to tell me her story. She had just gotten finished with Chemo - after five months of it. She had been battling Uterine cancer and Thyroid cancer - and she had been given a wonderfully positive prognosis.....so she and her hubby had decided that in order to celebrate her new life - they would adopt a dog together. The lady and her hubby stood holding each other and Buster and just beaming...."It's a new life for everyone," the husband said.

The husband looked at Buster and said "Would you like to come home with us? I promise you will be spoiled and loved. You can even sleep in bed with us!"

I watched as they put on the new collar and leash they had brought for Buster - adjusting it to fit him and getting him ready to put into the car. At the car door – Buster hesitated for a minute – and right on cue as if it were out of a Disney movie - Buster ran back to me - as if to say goodbye. I hugged him and kissed the little face that used to growl and bite in fear at me - so thankful that he had been rescued. He was a new dog now - and just like his new momma – he had been given a second chance.

"And I will give them singleness of heart and put a new spirit within them. I will take away their stony, stubborn heart and give them a tender, responsive heart," Ezekiel 11:19

"Thank You! Thank You!! Thank You!!!"

Duke was a beautiful five year old Male Boxer Dog. He came to us from a man whose son had Duke and had to give him up to move out of state. The man who surrendered him had him for several months but because Duke barked at his neighbor - the neighbor accused Duke of being a vicious dog (just for barking). Rather than the neighbor cause him lots of turmoil - he brought him to the rescue shelter to find him a home where Duke could be himself.....

The first thing I noticed about Duke was his mouth. Most boxers have pushed in snouts and long jowls that hang below their chins - but one side of Duke's mouth was pushed out.....His face looked a little like Elvis when he would twist his mouth and say "Thank you...Thank you very much!" Upon further examination - we found that Duke had a gingival hyperplasia tumor - common in Boxers...It was about the size of half a peach - growing just under his left front lip. It definitely impeded that way he would eat and seemed to cause him trouble drinking out of his bowl. He had a few other spots on his lower gum that were growing in the same way.

Worst of all - Duke did not accept much touching from us - ever! He always seemed guarded - like he was afraid we would bump his face. I could tell that the Duke we knew was not the Duke he could be....It was obvious that he was suffering from the lumps in his mouth.

We did not have a large amount of money in the coffers to pay for anything to be done for Duke. Surgery is not cheap. But it became obvious that with his mouth the way it was - and with the stand-offish manner he used to protect himself from pain - Duke would be difficult to place in a new home. My thoughts and prayers were often on this gorgeous boy who deserved a good home but needed to have this surgery......

As God would have it and just in time - we received some amazing donations from people in our community.... "Just because" donations that freed up other funds and were financially sizable enough to combine and to get the surgery done for Duke. I will never forget the morning that we loaded him into the minivan and took him to Soehnlen's Veterinary Clinic - where he was examined by Dr. Ditto...and in the same afternoon - he had the surgery to remove the tumors from his mouth. That day - he emerged from the recovery room - looking more handsome than ever. The "Elvis" look was gone.....and his face was smooth and perfect.

On the way home - he pushed his face into the wind out of the open window in the van - and once he was back at the Rescue - he followed me around for a while until the anesthesia wore off.....He kept pressing his face into my legs and putting his head in my lap - as if it was finally ok for him to be touched and held and loved. Each time I would stop and fall to my knees and cup his face in my hands and give him kisses on his forehead. He would look at me with his deep and serious eyes and just stare at me - as if to say "I don't know why you did this for me....but thank you! Thank you! Thank You!"

I was not the one who did anything other than what God would have me do for every one of the dogs in the rescue who needs fixed up, fixed, or who are suffering and need help. The help I can give them is limited – but usually any little thing helps....The donations of extra money for boarding, bags of food, tips given for grooming that are used for meds the shelter, and generous gifts from business people – those donations make this possible....Generous people make this a reality.

I was the one who was just lucky enough at that moment to hold Dukes sweet face in my hands and look into his eyes and see his gratitude - and his lack of frustration....I was able to see his pain transformed to appreciation.....

For all of the people who donate and do not get to be there for those moments - I needed to tell you about the difference you make....for Duke and for countless others who get their meds, who get fed, and for those whose pain is transformed to gratitude......Thank you! Thank You! THANK YOU!

"I do not cease to give thanks for you, remembering you in my prayers," Ephesians 1:16

"A Magnificent Dog"

I got a call from a fellow on Sunday morning...he asked me if we still had the dog available he'd seen on our website. The dog to which he was referring was Duke - the boxer. Duke had come to us from a guy who had to get rid of him because his neighbor thought that Duke "looked" and "sounded" vicious....and was making things at his neighborhood association tough on him....

Duke was also the Boxer who had surgery on his mouth while he was with us in the rescue. So Duke had become one of our favorites....a real winner and a wonderfully trained and beautiful dog.

So I asked the caller some important questions...."Have you ever owned a Boxer before?" The man's voice became soft "Oh yes - we have had six Boxers since I was just a little boy, " he began - and he told me a little bit about each one. The most recent one was Rocky "he was just six when he died of Cancer - in February of this year....it happened within a week...He was just a Magnificent Dog..." His voice trailed off and then he continued with his story "We had just brought him home from the vet because the vet said he had lymphoma and not much time. We brought him home to say goodbye to everyone - and we were all around him and just loving on him and he just died." His voice had dissolved into a whisper and I could hear him choking back the sadness that was still so raw.

So I spoke up and started telling him about Duke....while he regained his composure. I told him I'd send a picture of him so he could see how beautiful Duke really was...

I hung up with him and texted him a picture of our Duke...and he immediately texted me a picture back of his beloved lost Rocky from last summer - attached with the message – "I want Duke!! I want him for sure. He is perfect" He definitely was the perfect picture of Bob's old dog Rocky....They looked almost identical!! I knew it had to be more than a coincidence....

....So we made arrangements to meet him halfway between the shop and where they lived about an hour and a half away.....He told me "I will bring the whole family to welcome him into the pack."

At 1:30 on a Sunday afternoon - we met Bob, and Dee, and Michelle and Sarah....all there to welcome Duke. They were thrilled with him and he seemed so relaxed and happy around them....When they asked him if he wanted to come home with them - he perked up and became very animated....as if he knew exactly what the plan was.....He was so thrilled to be in the car, out of the rescue, and going home with a whole new family....

They say a picture is worth a thousand words...and later that day I received one....It was of Duke – laying out on the deck and over-looking the lake and basking in the sunshine of his new beautiful home!! No more neighbors to worry about....No more being left behind simply because of the way he looks or sounds....No worries because of his physical or medical needs.....The caption Bob put under his picture simply read: "Such a magnificent Dog. We are in love!" Us, too my friend – Love you forever Duke!!

"I have told you these things, so that in me you may have peace. In this world you will have trouble. But take heart! I have overcome the world." John 16:33

"In the Nick of Time"

Lynn's Golden Retriever dog, Zoom Zoom, had died at 13 of arthritis. "He just got down one day and couldn't get back up" she said. After the vet came out to put him down, Maggie - her 11 year old retriever and she were left to mourn him and miss him terribly. "Maggie has just never bounced back," She explained. "The only time she gets excited is when the grandkids come over...and then she wags her tail and seems a little bit happier. She doesn't greet me anymore when I get home. She is just so depressed."

Enter Sunny...A Golden Retriever that was dumped off in a remote area of Ohio by some people who obviously did not want to take care of him anymore and did not care that they were dumping him in the coldest week of the year!! I called him Sunny because he was in every way truly just a ray of Sunshine. He smiled all the time - and had such a happy and sweet personality....And though it was so cold – his happy little face just seemed to warm the hearts of everyone who saw him!

Still – he had been in the local pound for more than a month and no one seemed at all interested in him as a prospective pet....

He had obviously been someone's dog at one time because he was completely housebroken...he knew "sit" and "shake" and would even "Sit pretty" with his paws in the air. But his time was running out at the pound....His euthanasia date had been set....and I felt a stirring in my heart to help this doggie. When I went to get him - I knew for certain that I could place him easily because he was just so magnificent!

I called my sister - who has two golden retrievers of her own and teaches with an army of folks who own Goldens in the Pittsburgh - Washington, PA area. She always tells me - "If you get a Golden - check with me first!" She always knows people who are looking for companions for their own Goldens - or who have just lost one and are looking for another. Susan has helped me place five Goldens in the years I have been rescuing - and it just so happened that she helped me place Sunny. Lynn teaches with her at Washington-Jefferson University.-.and when she saw the picture I had sent Susan - Lynn said "Oh! - She looks just like my Maggie!!!"

I had planned to go to PA to take Sunny to Lynn or try to meet her halfway....but Lynn told me not to worry about it - and that she would like to come up to pick up Sunny. She was worried about him getting cold if she was late meeting us - and she wanted to drive him all the way back to bond with him. "My goal is to leave at 12:30 and be there to meet Sunny by 3:00, " She wrote to me the morning of his adoption – and at 2:50 - Lynn pulled in the driveway.

She walked around to the grooming room with me to meet Sunny - and he immediately greeted us both with kisses. We took him outside and he went potty and walked around with Lynn for a while – and she talked to him a bit about why she had come so far to get him.

Afterwards, I gave all of the information that I had about him to her… his shot records and his license…. Lynn got down close to Sunny and whispered to him "Are you ready to go home with me?" She asked – and just like that - he piled into her Subaru!!

He waited for her to get into the car, too - anxiously jumping from the front seat to the back seat - so excited to be going - somewhere....anywhere!!

Lynn let him jump around the car a bit and by the time she was backing out of my driveway - Sunny had himself positioned with his body standing on the back seat - and his head hanging over the front seat - right next to his new mom. The last thing I saw - as they drove down my street - was his big full tail - wagging vigorously - as if waving a thankful goodbye to me and looking ahead to his new life with Lynn and Maggie.

Lynn has promised pictures of the two of them once he and Maggie get acquainted - and I can only hope that he brings as much Sunshine to them as he did to everyone who met him here. And as for that stirring I felt in my heart to help him - I am so glad I listened to it. God no doubt had this mission planned out from the start....Saved in the nick of His perfect timing - so that Sunny and Lynn and Maggie could all rescue each other.

"For it is by grace you have been saved, through faith--and this is not from yourselves, it is the gift of God." Ephesians 2:8

"The Presence of Christmas "

My friend's sister's Pomeranian gave birth to a litter of puppies. One of them was born with what is sort of like the puppy version of Spina Bifida. He had an open scab on his back and the vet believed that some of the spinal fluid had leaked out and that the Nervous system was a bit under-developed or damaged somehow before birth. The puppy has developed normally with his brother and sisters - and has been completely healthy with one exception: he walks sideways. He also runs sideways...and sometimes - he falls down for no reason. His equilibrium is off and will probably never ever be 100% right on.

The prognosis for puppies of this sort is actually very good. They can live full lives...and often do - with the right people who will love them and care for them - and watch them carefully to be sure that they do not become injured due to falling.

My friend blessed me with the task of finding this very special puppy just the right home. And yesterday I am happy to say - that the little Pup found his life-long love in the arms of Shantalle – a little girl with some special needs of her own….

Shantalle's mom called me over the weekend and left a desperate message that she did not have much money but had seen some of my dogs on my website and wanted to know if there were any affordable puppies that she could purchase for her daughter for Christmas. "It is just the two of us - and I want to get her a dog...she has wanted a dog forever. They are all just so expensive!!" the mom said. So - I called the desperate mom back and told her about the little Pomeranian. I told her - He is full-blooded, beautiful and is going to stay tiny....he is just a little imperfect. I also told her he was "VERY" affordable as long as they would take good care of him and give him a good safe home.....

"Well he sounds perfect to me!" She said "I doubt if his feet will be touching the ground that often anyhow…I know my daughter - and she is going to carry that puppy around forever and never let him out of her sight!!"

We agreed to meet at the Walmart on Arlington Road in Akron - "My daughter will be the one standing in the middle of the parking lot flagging you down!" Shantalle's Mom said. She laughed - "She is going to just bust when I tell her about this!"

Sure enough - I pulled in the parking lot at the Walmart in our designated spot - and the little girl was standing beside the car and waving her hands vigorously. My heart skipped a beat. The smile on this little girl's face was priceless and I said to the tiny puppy "I really think your worries are over, little buddy!!"

In an amount of seconds - the little girl had the dog in her arms. And the mom had a matching smile of gratitude and tears because her daughter finally had the tiny puppy she had dreamed of giving her for Christmas. Best of all - they loved him - imperfections and all - with the kind of unconditional love that Christmas and it's "presence" are all about…Merry Christmas Shantalle & Tiny - and to the desperate mom who got exactly what she wanted for Christmas!!

"The earth and everything in it exists for the LORD— the world and those who live in it." Psalm 24:1

"From the Mouths of Babes"

They met me at McDonalds in Waynesburg...they had seen the little girl's picture on the website and had fallen in love with her. Their own dog had been hit by a car a year before and had to be put down...."This past year we made our yard more prepared for a dog. We put up a fence and made it all safe. Now we just need the dog," Leslie told me when she called to ask about the little Shih-Tzu-Bichon mix I had up for adoption.

"We have been looking for months...Every weekend....we go to the pounds - but they have so many pit-bulls ....that and we just don't want a big dog. My husband and the boys tease me about getting a big hunting dog - but we really just want one that we all agree on." she explained.

Leslie told me the minute she saw the little Shih-chon...she just knew. "I already showed my husband and he said 'Great! How soon can we get her?" Leslie explained that she wanted to meet me and the dog with everyone present - so we decided to meet at a halfway point at about 7pm.

My day was full up until then with grooming and rehoming two other dogs - but they wanted to see her as soon as possible. "The boys have been devastated since their little Pomeranian got hit by a car - I am sure when they see her they are going to just love her....but we want to make sure."

Leslie and Jim had three boys - a nine year-old and seven year-old twins. "They are all so different from each other. I know it is impossible to make everyone happy - but I want this to be the perfect place for her, too."

So we met at the halfway point – a McDonalds - at 7....Leslie and her husband, Jim, got out and the little shih-chon climbed into their waiting arms. "Does she have a name?" Jim asked. "No," I replied..."I have just been calling her little girl or baby" I told them.

"Good!" said Leslie "because they have been thinking of names all day!!"

Once Jim and Leslie had her in their arms - they opened the side door to the minivan and out popped three of most beautiful red-headed, freckle-faced boys I had ever seen...just bursting with orneriness - but at the moment looking like angels as they looked for the first time into the eyes of their new love.

"What do you think, Boys?" Leslie asked them.....In unison - their little heads bobbed up and down. "She is so cute!" said the oldest boy - leaning out over the other two to touch her carefully.

"She is really shy," Jim told them, "So no wrestling or rough-housing with her."

One of the twins looked at his dad and said "She is just a baby."

 The other twin looked at me very serious and said "She will get lots of love and we will be so careful with her."

I sensed that he was the "serious" twin. He stood a little off to the side and observed everything as it was going on. "You want to pet her?" Leslie asked the serious twin - and he shook his head "I'll let her come to me. I don't want to scare her."

For a moment - I watched from the sidelines - with the serious twin - as everyone just loved her and pet her - and she looked all around them - getting to know their smells and their faces. As they all piled back in the van - Jim asked them if they'd come up with a name yet.

"Maggy" They all said at the same time.

"Maggy" - it totally fit her. I watched the boys get into their seats and put Maggy between them. Just before the van door shut - the serious twin popped out and came over to me while I stood beside his parents. He put out his small gloved hand to me. I took it and he shook my hand. He looked me straight in the eyes and said "Thank you for what you do."

Bless his little heart. I got all teary eyed and tried to compose myself as I replied...."Oh honey - you are so welcome. Thank you for adopting Maggy."

It is a wonderful thing to see a dog get the blessing of a new home - especially with children who will love her....It is still yet another to know the child understands that this is a mutual blessing. I looked at his parents and said to them "Good job Mom and Dad - he totally gets it!"

With that - he gave me a little grin and disappeared into the van and sat somewhere in the darkness with his brothers and Maggy - all of them waiting to go home.

"But Jesus said, "Let the little children come to me and do not hinder them, for to such belongs the kingdom of heaven." Matthew 19:14

"Home Free"

Tonight Dino got a home! He was one of the very last dogs I had rescued from the Pound in October - and he had been here for what seemed like forever. I had several families look at him - and he was always "too small...too big....too hyper....too..."something" to be accepted for who he was and to be adopted.

And oh my - he needed a home!! So - with the threat of extremely cold weather coming this weekend - and not wanting to see this little guy get crowded out or have to get put out in the back room where it is cold - I did something that I NEVER do....I advertised him on Craigslist for just $35 and I and hoped and prayed for the best.

There are a million nut-jobs on there - and I held my breath - waiting for the crazy phone calls....but a half-hour after I listed him - I got a call from a nice lady named Beth in Kent who really loved his picture and wanted to adopt him. "The price is right, too" she said....She has a big family and they wanted a dog but did not want to spend an arm and a leg to get a good one. "Well - he is neutered and housebroken and ready to go!" I told her - and when I expounded on my information to tell her all about him - she said he seemed like the perfect dog for them!

We agreed to meet about an hour away from the rescue - but once there - I could not find her car. I called her and she told me she was having trouble getting her check cashed to get me my $35 - because she had not gotten out of work until late and that she might be late meeting me....
I told her "I'll tell you what - You come and get him and I'll waive the

fee...I really just wanted to make sure no crazy person on Craigslist was going to use him as Pitt Bull bait - that is why I put a fee on there, " I said.

She asked "Are you sure? I want to get you your money."

But I insisted. "Just Love him!" I told her - "that is payment enough."
15 minutes later, Beth rolled in with her four daughters...age 12 down to 18 months. Dino instinctively dove out of my Jeep and into their loving arms - going from child to child to child to Mom and giving them kisses of greetings and of thanks.

I gave Beth all of his accumulated stuff: leash to go with his collar, toys, blankie – vet records...and they put him in the car. Once in the car - he immediately went over and snuggled in the car seat with the 18 month old. We all laughed. "I told the girls when I picked them up from aftercare that we were going to get a surprise and that it was something alive...They were so excited - but did not know what it was until we got here."
The look on their faces was worth more to me than any money could have been - way more than $35 !!!

As I drove off - I could see their silhouettes in the car - Dino still going to each of them and offering kisses - and the girls all bouncing up and down in the car with delight. He was not "too anything" for them - except maybe too cute for words - because they mostly squealed with excitement that he was really theirs. Way to go Dino!! You are finally HOME!!

"The blessing of the Lord makes rich, and he adds no sorrow with it."
Proverbs 10:22

"The Calling"

Yesterday - a woman called me about one of the dogs on my web site that was already adopted. I told her the dog had already found a good home - but that I would be very happy to take her number and if another one came along - I would call her. She seemed skeptical that I could or I would do that.

I told her - "No - I actually have people saved in my cell phone who have specific needs or wishes for a rescue dog - who have been qualified as a good adopter - and I will call if the right dog for them comes along."

She then asked me "Well, How long does it take?"

This made me smile. In my head - I thought - well if you are looking for an adult black lab mix....or a pit-bull -I could find you one in just a few seconds....but I politely responded "Oh -sometimes a week or two - sometimes just a few days. Life at the rescue is like a box of chocolates....I never know what I am going to get."

We then exchanged some really good conversation...and I told her way too much about my life - and how I became a dog rescuer....I listened to her talk about the dog she had recently lost and how she longed for another baby to love and cuddle. I also told her not to be discouraged by the fact that the dog she fell in love with on the website was already adopted.

"That just means that God will be saving the right baby for you at the right time." I said.

By the time we hung up - we were both laughing had had an extremely good time talking about our dogs, the Lord, and how blessed we both were to have spoken to each other just then. She said to me "I am encouraged. I am so glad that I called. It seemed to be just the right thing. I needed this - this morning. God Bless you - I will wait on your call."

As I hung up and paused to put her name in my phone - along with the dozen or so others who had given me their names over the weekend with their wish lists for doggies - I suddenly realized that God had placed in me a frighteningly huge responsibility. I had the names of hurting people in my phone who were waiting for me to find them a love that would heal them. I had the divine charge of looking for a warm and cuddly body and cold nose that would bring unconditional love to a family or home. I guess I never thought about it much before -because I always put everything in God's hands and just thought I was lucky or blessed to be able to deliver the goods. But yesterday it hit me...Just as I had chosen God so many years before - God had chosen me to be the matchmaker of cuddles, of healing tail wags, and wet puppy kisses ...

Not that this makes me feel any more powerful or interesting....but I did for a moment feel a chill of the Holy Spirit run through me - and I bowed my head to thank my Heavenly Father for trusting me with this ministry.

It is an amazing feeling - those moments that we realize that our profession is a calling...and that our efforts are a "bestowed" privilege - chosen for us by the God who loves us. And truly anything any of us do - can be done in His name - if we seek Him and chose Him as the Leader of our lives. Work can truly become a way of sharing His unconditional love and bearing witness to His miracles in our lives.

"You are a chosen people. You are royal priests, a holy nation, God's very own possession. As a result, you can show others the goodness of God, for he called you out of the darkness into his wonderful light." 1 Peter 2:9

"Two much love!"

When Lori adopted Layla from me - we both thought she was not going to be a very big dog. She was supposed to be a Mini Border Collie and small Terrier Mix. When she got her she was 11 weeks old and still very tiny. I do not know if - like Clifford the Big Red Dog - Lori's love for Layla made her grow unusually large - or if the lady whose mini Border Collie got impregnated fingered the wrong mutt as the father...but Layla got a lot bigger than either of us expected.

Unfortunately - at 8 months - Layla was already too big for her Mobile Home - AND the rules at her trailer park where a dog in residence there can be no larger than 20 pounds. Lori contacted me tearfully - and when I finally had room for Layla - she found herself back in the same rescue room where her young life began.

Layla had grown up to be a little skittish - typical Border Collie Behavior - high strung - always trying to herd me. She also looked like she might have a little Greyhound in her. She was sleek and built for speed. She really just needed to have a place to run - and once she got in my back yard - I ran her around and she kicked up her heels. She had the ability to jump straight up in the air on all fours - and she never left the yard. She was a pleasant surprise. I know Lori was probably really frustrated trying to keep her busy in her confined environment. This dog just needed space - and neither of us could help that Layla had turned out to be a rambunctious and larger dog than we had expected.

It was not Lori's fault. She really did a good job with Layla because Layla was a really good dog! She listened well and was already housebroken.

I advertised Layla as a Border Collie/Greyhound mix - because I wanted prospective adopters to know she needed to have a place to run. She found herself on my website page with three tiny little Poms and Chihuahuas competing for homes. I never thought that she would be the first to get adopted!! But Late Friday - I got a call from a sweet elderly gentleman named Larry and his wife Sharon who already had a greyhound/collie mix and were hoping to add another to their "Zoo" "We have a little bit of everything...Cats, snakes, a McCaw..." the wife said on the phone, giggling. "She'll fit right in!"..... "We have two acres - fenced in - so Layla will have the run of the place. I'll bet she'll like that!" Larry said. We made plans to meet on Saturday at 1 pm.

I bathed Layla and got her all beautiful. I told her that her new family was waiting to take her home. I let her out to go to the bathroom....and then put her in a crate in the van because she jumped around in the car before - and I was afraid she'd hurt herself. Unfortunately - all of my primping of Layla was for not....because once in the crate - Layla let go of some nervous loose pooh and by the time we got to Larry and Sharon - it was like she was shake and baked in her own goods.

She smelled horrible - she was slimy....and I was very very apologetic. I wiped her down with towels and told Larry to take her over in the snow and get her a little wet so we could wipe her off some more. "This will give them time to bond!" - Sharon said....And Layla was already kissing Larry's face as he wiped her off and kissed her right back......I again said I was so sorry she was such a sloppy mess...

The whole poopy thing might have bothered some people – but it didn't seem to matter to them at all. They kissed her on the top of her head - and hugged her even in her poopy places. Sharon had brought a blanket and

43

wrapped it around her and took her in the back seat and sat next to her. Larry assured me it was fine with them. "When you love as many animals as we do - a little pooh is to be expected." He smiled

As Larry got into the car - and they drove off with Layla - I saw her settle in next to Sharon. Sharon wrapped her arms around a very smelly Layla and gave her a warm hug and they exchanged more kisses. I stood smiling and waving with a knot in my throat and happy tears rising up in my eyes. If they could love her right away in this condition, I thought, then certainly she would wrap them around her paws forever. And with the love they will show her - combined with the love that Lori had given her - she would probably grow a little bigger still.

"You did not choose me, but I chose you and appointed you so that you might go and bear fruit—fruit that will last—and so that whatever you ask in my name the Father will give you." John 15:16

"Jackie"

We lived together for several months - after having been dropped off at my house in February with her sister by some nice folks who just couldn't keep them any longer. The sister got a home after a while - but as a senior citizen doggie - and a Jack Russell to boot - Jackie faced an uncertain future - and I knew that....So I decided to keep her - until God decided her true fate.

I am a big fan of Jack Russell Terriers for several reasons - They are loud - like me....They are extremely adaptable - like me....and they don't wait for anyone to help them do anything - they just figure out a way to get what they want - like me. Jackie was no exception....She was nine years old - but still moved like a young pup. She hunted, she burrowed, and she loved to walk miles and miles with me in a day.....In fact – one day – a little yorkie ran away from my shop and I spent the entire day walking the streets of East Sparta looking for her - Jackie walked every mile with me - never tiring of our apparent mission. I loved Jackie from the start .....

But she also liked to bark at traffic and at children and birds on our street - She was just doing her job - she thought. But she often woke up my family - and as soon as we moved the rescue from the back of our home to the new grooming shop - she moved there to guard it full time.

Unfortunately - as my time became more and more limited and the business began to get busy - I realized that what Jackie needed was a home.....less busy...and more lazy. It is a funny thing - when you love something with the kind of love that God intended us to have for each other - you cannot be selfish in that love. Even though I loved Jackie with

45

my whole heart - I could not keep her in a place where she was restricted or uncomfortable. I had to think of her - and had to find a place for her where she could be free to be Jackie.....

One Monday night - Jackie's opportunity came in the form of a girl named Rachael....She actually showed up to the rescue to see another dog - a Jack Russel mix named Gidget....Rachael liked Gidget - but She began asking us if we had something a little older, a little more settled...."I really have a soft spot for the senior citizen dogs because no one wants them.....and I love Jack Russells.....Do you have any of them?" My wonderful volunteer and helper Christine and I looked at each other and said "Oh! Jackie!" In minutes - Jackie was getting acquainted with her future new momma.....it was truly love at first sight.

I even had the opportunity to give Jackie a bath before she left - and the whole time I told her how much I loved her and how this was definitely a positive step for her future...She gave me kisses and seemed to understand.....When she was all ready to go - I handed her over to her new mom and she promised to keep us informed of her new life.

I am usually glad to see the doggies go from the rescue - and this time I was thrilled for Jackie - but had the biggest lump in my throat....I watched as she jumped into Rachael's car - hopped up in the passenger seat and drove away....

Hours later - I got a text from Rachael tell me that they took a long walk, they went to the Pet Store and she got a new "girlie" wardrobe and she sent me a picture of her sleeping in her new collar.....The lump in my throat turned to a soaring in my heart for Jackie - I knew that night she would sleep in a bed - snuggled beside her new momma...and I was reminded by God of the unselfish reasons that we do what we do....

The next morning - Rachael sent me another text - "She slept next to me all night...she is doing just great! Oh - by the way - She snores and farts...it's like I adopted another boyfriend!!" I showed the text to my Rescue family and we all laughed!! Of course I already knew this about Jackie....after all - We lived together for several months - having been dropped off in February. I love you Jackie - and I'll never forget our time together! So glad to give you a happy beginning.....Kisses!

"Love is patient and kind; love does not envy or boast; it is not arrogant or rude. It does not insist on its own way; it is not irritable or resentful; it does not rejoice at wrongdoing, but rejoices with the truth. Love bears all things, believes all things, hopes all things, endures all things. Love never ends. " I Corinthians 13:4-7

"A Mother's Love – Part 1"

They were found walking down Rt. 43 in Carrollton....A Momma Dog and 7 babies....Two of her litter had been struck and killed - another one was found later and got a different home....but the remainder of this little family - 7 puppies and their momma - found their way to our Rescue last week....and their journey – as one of our favorite rescue families - began.

The first thing we noticed about this little family was just how incredibly wonderful the momma dog was. Lucy - the name we gave to the momma - was always checking on her puppies and playing with them - but she also gave them room to grow and learn on their own....She didn't hover - but often watched them from across the room - giving them time to settle on their own - but always nearby so that she could intervene if they got too upset.

We also fell in love with her amazing gentle and loving nature she had with all of us. Lucy trusted us almost immediately - and she gave unconditional love generously....Lucy was always finding her way onto our laps - and into our hearts...Lucy was just a love - and everyone who met her loved her right away!!

Because Lucy's Pups were so beautiful and every bit as sweet as she - they began to get homes pretty quickly....This was alright with Lucy - because she knew instinctively that her babies were made to grow up and be loved by families of their own....The only thing that Lucy ever demanded was involvement in the adoption process....and we granted her this opportunity freely....

So when Terri - the Police officer came to adopt one of the female puppies as an anniversary gift for his wife - Lucy gave her approval and watched proudly as he got his picture taken with her when he came to pick her up.....And when Darrell - the teacher bought a fluffy male puppy for his fiance' - Lucy jumped up to give her little boy a goodbye kiss before they departed for their new home with the big fenced back yard in Greentown.....And - when Cheyenne came all the way from Lake Milton to pick out a little boy puppy for she and her boyfriend's first house together - Lucy gave both Cheyenne and the little boy puppy a kiss of approval and joy that yet another of her babies was bound for a happy future and a great life of their own.

As Cheyenne started to leave with the puppy - one of our visitors asked us if it might be hard for the momma dog to watch her babies leave - one by one....We remarked that it probably was - because up until the time of adoption - they had all been so close....But Lucy made this so much easier on all of us - and on her children because - as a wonderful, trusting, and loving mother - she did not love her children selfishly - but surrendered them to their individual lives with an open heart -with the selfless love and faith that all amazing moms seem to possess....and the ability to know that loving completely means eventually kissing them goodbye and letting them go.

"Lo, children are an heritage of the Lord: and the fruit of the womb is his reward" Psalms 127:3

"A Mother's Love – Part 2"

The last one left tonight....The last black puppy that came in with the Momma Dog Lucy two weeks ago....A very nice couple came in with their little girl to look at a few dogs and they fell in love....The last puppy had originally been chosen by another couple - but they later had changed their minds for one of our older and tougher pups for their boys....leaving this last one still at the rescue to be with the Momma for a few days more.....The couple knew it was the last to leave....and they felt really sorry for Momma. I explained that she had taken the other adoptions like a trooper - and as long as she got to play with each pup and kiss it goodbye before it left - she was at peace.....

Fortunately - the couple had to go down the street to the ATM for cash for the adoption fee - and Momma made every moment with this little girl puppy count.....She played and rolled with her - and cleaned her one last time. By the time the couple got there - Momma and the pup were on the floor together - and I had to pick up the puppy from beside Momma and hand it to the couple as they signed their agreement papers and walked out the door....I followed them out to thank them and make sure they got on their way ok.

"Oh - the Momma is giving me the eye - " Said the puppy's new human, Michael....I looked up to see Momma looking stoically out the window at them as they turned with her baby to leave.....their little girl looked at me and said "Thank you for getting me my puppy !!!" I smiled and nodded to Momma in the window and said - "Oh - she is the one responsible for that!".....and as Momma stood there starring at the sweet little family - the little girl touched the window - just in time for Momma to lick her little hand through the glass....."Thank you for giving me my puppy!" She called to Momma through the window.....And at that - Momma jumped down from her perch by the door and settled somewhere in the front room on the floor....

They were pulling away and I sat down on one of the chairs by the lunch table - a few feet away from Momma....She got up and put her head in my lap - then eased herself up and rested her head on my shoulder as I hugged her and my eyes filled with tears....."You did it Momma - they all got great homes and you did such a great job!" We snuggled there for a second - and before I knew it - she had crawled all the way into my lap and was a little ball cradled in my arms....

Her role of Momma was done - and she sought nothing now but the love and comfort of her human family to soothe her losses and secure her uncertain future...."Since you don't have to be a Momma anymore - you can just be a baby....our baby!" I told her....And as I kissed her cheek - she sighed - a big and bittersweet sigh...I held her there for a long time with our foreheads pressed together - rocking back and forth with my tears falling down on her. For I know what it is to have the little ones grow up and leave...I knew her thoughts at that moment -and we sat there in the front room of the rescue - and at the same time felt rescued and in need of a rescue....It is always so good to see all of our children doing so well - but it is always hard to see the last one go...Tonight was a little tough....the last one left tonight.

"Train up a child in the way he should go; even when he is old he will not depart from it." Proverbs 22:6

"The Great Gift"

They dated as kids....in high school...and were crazy about each other. They went to Proms and Homecoming Dances....but their love did not last into adulthood and took the path of most high school romances....It became - for them - a fond memory.

They both grew up, married other people and had separate lives and families. They both experienced the joy of raising their children, of welcoming grandchildren, and they both lived through the bitter-sweet reality of divorce. After 37 years of not seeing each other and living life separately, they found each other on Facebook ....They began talking, then meeting, and after 37 years - they rekindled something that they both were unable to eradicate from their past: Their love for one another.

Karen and Ted enjoyed a beautiful relationship in their golden years....even more wonderful than the one they had shared as kids....."Because we had done all of the hard work," Karen said "We were able to just sit back and enjoy each other." Karen described it as a "great gift". She said they moved around a bit - and finally settled an agreeable distance between all of their kids so that they could visit them all equally.

Ted was on disability because he had developed COPD "From smoking..."Karen said "But I got him to quit smoking the second year we were together.....but of course the damage was already done." Yes - unfortunately Ted developed pneumonia this past spring and after being together a much shorter time than they should have been in the middle of these golden years together, Ted passed away very suddenly. Karen was devastated, understandably. She called us three weeks after Ted had passed, telling us that she found our rescue on-line, and she wanted to get a small dog for company.

Funny thing was, she came looking for a girl dog....She said she wanted a yorkie. We showed her several of the yorkies we had...but it was not until we brought out the boy yorkie that she really perked up. She fell in love instantly....and we think the doggie did, too...Once she picked up the little tri-colored yorkie who we had been calling "Burger" - her heart melted - and Burger snuggled onto her chest and put his little face over her shoulder.

My Best friend Christine - who was at the shelter helping out that day said to Karen "Look at how he just snuggled up to you! That is amazing!!" and Karen smiled at us...and said "I think this one knows how much I need him." Then she looked at him and asked him the million-dollar question that all dogs in rescue long to hear...."Do you want to go home with me?" Burger wagged his entire body and she handed him to us and said "This is the one."

After a little celebration and hugs between us, Karen said "Maybe I bonded with the boy dog because.....I miss him so much" she said of her husband..."And I know he would want me to be happy.....and this little guy is going to bring me much happiness....so I am going to call him Teddy....name him after Ted." Karen said.....and the tears she had fought back through this entire meeting fell everywhere around her. Chris and I joined her in a good little cry....

There was just so much emotion in the room at that moment....as if God stood between Ted - the husband in heaven - and Karen - the widow on earth - and had joined us all in a circle of love with this amazing little needy pup in the middle.....

"That is just perfect." Chris said......

"I am happy for you and Teddy" I said....

Chris and I disappeared shortly to the back room to give "Teddy" a bath and get him all ready for his trip home with his new lady - smelling all good to start his new life.

"Can you imagine?" Chris said - helping me scrub the sweet little guy. "I know!" I replied....We stood there rinsing Teddy and lost in our own thoughts about what had just happened.....Our cheeks were still moist from our cry with Karen and the little dog between us stood perfectly still and waited for us to finish and hand him off to his blessed new life. We knew that he would experience good fortune like he had never known - because he was supplying a need - and filling a hole in Karen's heart. We knew that we had just experienced a touch of the Holy Spirit and yet another "Great Gift" from beyond....and that Teddy and Karen were going to live out some wonderful golden years together.

"And my God will supply every need of yours according to his riches in glory in Christ Jesus." Philippians 4:19

"Togetherness"

They came in together.....They had been thrown out of a moving car in Carroll County....They were brother and sister - bonded by whatever they had been through as young pups and through their quick trip to the pavement from the jerk who used to be their "dog parent"......The person who rescued them had actually witnessed this "Dumping" - grabbed up the doggies from the road - chased the Dog Dumper to the county line and got some of their license numbers written down. Then he took the dogs to the Dog Pound and reported the incident.....

Thankfully - the Deputy Warden, Laura, had the presence of mind to call us and tell us about them - knowing that they needed more than to be put into a cell at the Pound...They needed TLC for their road rash and needed to be in a safe and caring environment that would nurture them to trust humans and show them that all humans were not going to hurt or abandon them. So we went directly to the pound and adopted them - took them back to the rescue - and their long stay with us began - in June - shortly after 'Here Doggie Doggie Rescue' opened its doors.

Champ and Honey came into the Rescue - shaking, bloody, and scared. They had some definite scrapes from falling to the pavement - and they absolutely refused to be out of each other's sight for more than a few seconds.....We all decided that it would probably be best to keep them - and re-home them together - even if it meant waiting a long time for the right adopter to come along. We all knew this would be difficult - since it is sometimes impossible to re-home two dogs - bonded pairs. People do not usually want two dogs at once...But we put it in God's hands and tried to have faith that they would get adopted together....Someday.......We hoped.

Champ and Honey thrived in the rescue environment, for I fear it was better than anything they had experienced. They ate together, slept together, cuddled together and learned to trust us and love us as their caretakers. We had lots of people ask us if we would separate them, because prospective adopters wanted one or the other...and often we considered it just to get them both homes....But we knew they would both be heartbroken if they did not remain together....and we stayed committed to our plan of keeping them together...We continued to trust...We continued to Hope....

.

One sunny Friday - I received an email from a woman named Becky....It read: "Our little mixed breed mutt, Harry, lost his two best friends because our daughters moved out of the house this summer and took their dogs with them. We were relieved that the house would be quiet without all of the commotion of our children and their pets, but we now find that our Harry is just beside himself and mourning the loss of his buddies. I am interested in the bonded Chihuahua mix pair you have on your website....What can you tell me about Champ and Honey?"

My heart took a leap and I asked Becky to call me as soon as possible. A few hours later - I was on the phone with her - and knew right away she was the right person!!

She was funny - easy going - and loved her dog more than herself.....Her husband was on board for the adoption "Anything for little Harry," He'd said! So Saturday - Christine and I met with the lady and delivered the two little bonded Chihuahuas to her. What was funny was that they acted like they had known Becky all of their lives....They jumped into her car and made themselves at home on the two doggie baskets she had fashioned in the front seat....Honey kept giving her kisses - and Champ just seemed so full of JOY to be headed somewhere with his sister.....We watched as they all drove away - so excited and relieved that they had gotten a home together!!

This morning - I got this email from Becky "I just wanted to say Thank-you for meeting me with the bonded pair! Our first day together wasn't too bad. Our trip to the dog park didn't go as well as I hoped. Honey was the problem. She just was very grumpy to dogs & people both. I sat and held her which helped a little but we decided to leave thinking maybe Honey was stressed with everything so new around her. Now Champ and my dog Harry get along great and things there are wonderful. My dog Harry is doing better already. I'm so happy that my dog and cat both seem to like Champ. And Honey is fine so long as she is being held or within eyesight of Champ.....They are the best dogs for all the new things that were thrown at them and so loving, and very well house broken. I can't Thank you enough! Thanks again, Becky."

Thank YOU Becky - for giving our little bonded pair a great new home! I know that they will never again be dumped or abandoned - and I know that they rescued your little Harry right back from him missing his old companions... Way to Go Champ and Honey!! Our hopes were answered by a forever together home for you both!!

"The Lord is good to those who wait for him, to the soul who seeks him."
Lamentations 3:25

"A Plan in the Making"

They came for her late in the summer, Liz and her boy....they wanted him to have a dog of his own...Liz already had a fluffy little lap dog that was her baby - but Josh, her son - needed a boy's dog....a dog he could train and play rough with - and a dog that would be his best friend in the growing up years....a "Man's best friend" dog that he would remember for the rest of his life. After hearing about Sophia, the Shepherd - Rot mix whose career as a service dog had been cut short by her owner's illness - they decided to come for her...

Sophia was a wonder dog - of sorts. She was very young when her owner began training her as a service dog. Sophia already knew lots of commands, was housebroken. Her owner and trainer became ill, however, and Sophia was turned over to us....Liz and her son decided to give her a home. But their "surprise" in bringing Sophia home was taken by Liz's Husband as more of a sneaky way of getting another dog in the house and he told them he they had to return the dog....and with tears from all of us - she was taken back into the rescue....

I remember all of us that were there that day sitting and praying as Liz and her boy left the rescue "Please God - soften that Daddy's heart so that Josh can have Sophia" "Please give some reasoning behind that little boy's tears...We know you have your reasons...."

Well - as fate would have it - God had lots of reasons for Josh to not take Sophia at that time.....4 to be certain.....Sophia was pregnant! She had come to the rescue that way - and just a few short weeks after Liz and Josh had come for her and returned her - Sophia gave birth to 11 puppies - 4 of which lived....Sophia was a great mom and she doted on her litter of babies....However - she was young and the movement from her owner's home to the shelter had stressed her and caused her milk production to be low...She really only had enough to feed the 4 strong babies who survived.

When news of the puppies reached Liz - she said "Well now that would not have gone over very well at all in our house!" She laughed "Everything happens for a reason I guess!"
It certainly does...As luck would have it - as soon as Sophia's puppies started eating hard food - she became strong and willful again...It became apparent to us at the rescue that she would need a good home....My friend Christine and I said "if only that little boy could come back for her! She really needs a home now that the pups are not eating from her!"
Oddly enough - God was already working on this plan.....Late in the evening on October 31st - while Chris and I were at a Halloween party - I received a text from Liz...."Todd said for us to come get Sophia...Out of the Blue - I am so excited!!!" I texted back "She is ready!! Come tomorrow!"

Sure enough - the busy busy Saturday morning came and Liz and Josh and her other son came in the door to re-claim the prize that God had held for them for so long - the one He intended for them to have - but in His time....Because I was so busy - they had to wait just a bit while I bathed and dried Sophia....She kept looking at Josh as I held her back to dry her - and once she was finally ready - she danced around both of them - as if she knew in her heart that they would be coming back for her....And as Josh and Sophia wrestled around and she licked Liz's face - I said a thank you to God and knew this was always meant to be....

Later that day I received a text from Liz with pictures of Josh and Sophia Playing and even later a text saying "Success! Sophia is sleeping on Josh's bed tonight! Thank You Thank You!" Thank God - for He knew the Plan and had Josh's Best Friend's Happy Beginning in His hands all along.

"Trust in the Lord with all your heart, and do not lean on your own understanding. In all your ways acknowledge him, and he will make straight your paths." Proverbs 3:5-6

"A Good Friday"

The other morning when I posted the pictures of Puppies on our Facebook Page, I was contacted almost immediately by a woman named Richelle. The message I received from her was long and I read it as her story unfolded in my Facebook PM window. Richelle's Family's 15 year old dog had died in August. This had been their son Hunter's only dog - because he was just 10 years old. They mourned the passing of their pet for a while before deciding to get another dog....and over the winter adopted a beautiful yellow lab and beagle mix from a rescue in the Dover area. The adoption process was long and they waited for their puppy while the rescue did background checks and placement testing. Hunter was so excited when they finally got to bring their puppy home!!

But a day or so after the puppy arrived, the puppy got sick. And despite the efforts of an excellent vet and lots of tears and prayers - the puppy died. Hunter was crushed and Richelle and her husband were devastated. They did not really know what to do - but they knew Hunter needed a buddy...and so they were willing to try again when just the right puppy came along.

I agreed to meet Richelle and Hunter at the shop where the puppies were Friday morning. Ironically - this Friday was Good Friday....the Friday before Resurrection Sunday. I thought about that as I drove to the shop to meet them. Their little pup had passed, and they were lost without it. It had brought back the pain of losing their old dog and they found themselves in a sadness for which there seemed to be no end. They were in need of a miracle....I only hoped that one of those pups would be that miracle.

When I met them - I was so impressed. Richelle was just an awesome lady - with spunk and humor and a light in her eyes. Hunter as a bit more reserved - which tickled me because they reminded me of myself and my son Sam when he was little. The child - so serious and quiet - and the mom so bubbly and talkative.

They waited in the front room as I brought out armloads of puppies for them to see. 10 in all. Hunter looked carefully and held a few of them, but then picked out the boy puppy that I knew would probably be the one - a little tan and yellow pup who was chubby and sweet and the most beautiful of the boy pups. Hunter settled in a chair and held the squirming puppy and we let it down on the floor as it ran around and kept coming back to Hunter to play.

As we watched Hunter interact with the pup - Richelle recounted the days of losing their puppy and explained how worried they were about getting another one. Tears in her eyes fell from her face - and though it had been a little while - I knew her pain was still fresh. I watched Hunter playing with the puppy carefully and knew that this might just be the one. She kept asking him to be sure and they decided that this was definitely the one. They wanted to wait a day - just to talk it over - and later in the afternoon - she sent me a happy message and confirmed that they would be coming for the puppy in the morning.

I cannot tell you what it feels like to deliver a puppy into the waiting arms of a child and seeing the happy tears in the eyes of a mom who only wants happiness and healing for past pain in her son. But I can tell you - it feels awesome. When they picked up that little puppy on Saturday - I felt an amazing thankfulness to God that this puppy could bring so much joy - and that I could be the one to help them find it. I watched them carefully take the pup into their car and the happy puppy innocently licking Hunter's face and bouncing all over Richelle - and I knew immediately that this was a Resurrection Story.

Their pain and love for the other dogs could never be erased - but this puppy had come to fill the holes in their hearts with kisses and tickles and love. He had turned their Pain and Sorrow into Hope and Joy. He was Hunter's new best friend - and had come just in time for Easter. Happy Easter Hunter, Richelle, her hubby and the new puppy now named Rocky!!!

"For I am sure that neither death nor life, nor angels nor rulers, nor things present nor things to come, nor powers, nor height nor depth, nor anything else in all creation, will be able to separate us from the love of God in Christ Jesus our Lord." Romans 8:38-39

"An Emptiness Fulfilled"

When I rescued the four five-year old labs from a breeder in Southern Ohio, I was lucky enough to have Shirley in the bunch of them. Shirley was the charcoal lab, a beautiful girl who had obviously been used for producing lots of puppies. She was by far the most needy, and she would always stand right in front of me - with her eyes fixed on my face, tail wagging slowly, and peering into my eyes with a look that said "Love me....Just love me." I often did just that. Taking my hands and running them over her ears and kissing her - she would make all sorts of happy noises and her tail would wag faster. When I stopped - she would not jump or whine like lots of dogs do - but would patiently just stand and start looking at me again with that expression in her eyes that would make me want to give her more lovins - right away.

Shirley and her sister Labs were all very good dogs, but Shirley was special. She never left my side when we walked outside, and she just seemed to have a spirit that had been somehow injured or duped by fate. It seemed that she had looked for love and a forever home in her past, but had been shifted around, moved from place to place and had always come up short and alone. I hoped that wherever she landed - she would get to be the only dog and she would get all of the lovins for the rest of her life.

Enter Jack - an elderly man from Leesville who I came in contact with through a Deputy Dog Warden Named Laura. Jack had called her pound looking for a companion dog because his dog had died recently. Laura said "He had wanted something like a blue tick or a heeler - but call him if you have one you think will be good for him." I immediately knew it had to be Shirley.

63

So I called Jack the same day I got his number - and told him all about Shirley. "I know you were looking for something a little different, but I really think she might just be a good fit for you"....and then I went on to tell him all about Shirley's attributes and what a good dog she was. Jack did not bite immediately. He told me he needed time to think about it....but five minutes later - the phone rang and it was Jack - calling me back to tell me he didn't want to lose out on this opportunity - and he would meet me in the afternoon to meet Shirley.

Sure enough - at 4:30 sharp - I pulled into the Park that was halfway between our homes where we had agreed to meet. Jack already had the back seat of his car fashioned for a companion - sheets over the back seat - a blanket and a pillow, and a lead ready to walk her. He said "Let's get in the car together so she isn't afraid." So I sat with Jack for a while in the front seat while Shirley hung her head between us over the seat and got acquainted with Jack.

While we were sitting there - Jack told me that his wife had passed a few years ago - and that his old dog Jesse had been his best friend and companion ever since. He said "Jesse, died on March 7, and I swore I'd never put myself through that again." His eyes filled with tears as he continued: "I am 77 years old and I didn't want a puppy who was going to outlive me - and how do you get a dog that is gonna be like the one you just lost? I didn't even want to try again. But in two weeks, I was tired of being alone. I have hills and trails all over my property." He swallowed hard and tears fell down his cheeks..."And you get tired of walking alone."

I was in tears, too - and we both became quiet for a moment.....Shirley instinctively jumped into the front seat as if to comfort us both. This made us both laugh and we had to get out and put her back in the back seat again. I'd better get her home before she does that again. She looks like a real sweetheart." Jack said. "Thank you Rita, I will let you know how we get along."

Since that day - I have received daily emails from Jack. Jack and Shirley have gotten along quite well. Shirley sleeps in the bed with Jack every night. They go on long walks around the lake and all over his property and in his own words "She never leaves my side. I don't even need a leash with her. She just wants to be with me...wherever I go. Never have I had one that just walks beside me - that I don't have to keep tethered. I never have to chase her - She is just the perfect companion....my friend and my sweetie. She is not at all what I was looking for - but she is even better than I expected!"

Obviously - Shirley has found her forever home and is getting all of the lovins - and will for the rest of her life....and both she and Jack will never again have to walk alone.

"Delight yourself in the Lord, and He will give you the desires of your heart." Psalm 37:4

"No Name"

"Shih-Chon" - the little curly white and black Shih Tzu - Bichon Mix who was in the rescue this week - had lived most of her life in a 30 x 30 inch crate. Her job in life was to procreate....make babies for her owners - and be a good momma. Unfortunately for her owner - she did not do such a great job with all of that!! "Shih-Chon" (called that because she never had a proper name either) had been bred at such a young age that she destroyed her babies every time she had a litter. Therefore - she found herself fired.....kicked out of her crate and her farmer's life....She came to me with milk still in her teets and a homeless doggie with a sad past and an uncertain future.....Luckily - God already had plans for "Shih Chon".... After viewing her on my website, a wonderful lady named Stephanie contacted me about adopting her for her 87 year old mom. Her mother had lost her dog several years ago and had waited to get another dog because she was afraid that she would not outlive a new pet.

Stephanie told me - at the time that her mom had lost her own dog -"We had a Shih Tzu and my sister had a Lhasa Apso, so she didn't want to burden us with another dog if she died first." But Stephanie said - "Time has passed and my mom is still in good health. My Shih Tzu has died and my Sister's Lhasa has died - so now we all miss the company of a dog.....Mom lives with my sister now - so if anything happens - the dog will have a home no matter what."

I told her all about "Shih chon – how she had been used for breeding and how she had never had a proper name or a home…"I just cannot understand it," Stephanie said "No name? How is a dog supposed to know

66

it is alive? How horrible!" She said...."I want my mom to meet this dog with no name!"

So on Saturday evening - at 5:30 - I met these three beautiful women halfway between our homes and of course, they all fell in love with little "Shih-Chon". The two doting daughters lifted her from her place in the back of my van and placed her on their 87 year-old momma's lap.... Sophia, their mother – took her on her lap and the daughters watched carefully as she started to pet her and look into her eyes. Sophia grinned and looked up at her daughter's with knowing and delighted tears in her eyes and wrapped her arms around the sweet little dog – who had lived in a cold box just a few weeks ago....Slowly – "Shih-Chon" relaxed and snuggled against the elderly woman's coat - then put her head against Sophia's heart....Sophia just kept petting her and "Shih-Chon" just kept melting deeper and deeper into her lap.

By the time "Shih-Chon" had almost drifted off to sleep – the sisters were thinking of names for this little orphan who obviously just wanted a home so desperately. I could see that "Shih-Chon" had sealed the deal with her sweetness and her need for love. The three women would be taking her to a place where she would be loved and nurtured for the rest of her life. Never again would she have to have puppies just to be kept and fed....and never again would she be fired from the only secure place she had ever known. Her job in life now was just to love and be loved....she would now have a name and a forever family....and she was finally home.

"Fear not, for I have redeemed you; I have called you by name, you are mine." Isaiah 43:1

"A Long Time Coming!"

She had been there the longest....she was there, at the rescue, before the water and electricity were turned on, and before people were walking in off the streets to adopt dogs.....She saw over 200 dogs get adopted...She was there to see puppies be born and a few old doggies pass away. She was a favorite of visitors and staff, family and volunteers......She was passed over so many times - and we all felt for her - prayed for her to get a home....and were often frustrated and sad for her....But last night she finally got to sleep in a real bed - with a real mom and dad....who knew before they ever met her that she was the dog for them.....

She had been there for what seemed like forever – but Chloe - the longest resident of the rescue - finally got a home!!!

Chloe came in with her brother, Shortie - a dachshund mix - who was adopted out very quickly because of his small size and his immediate charm. Chloe was the larger and quieter of the two...she came to us already spade and housebroken and she had a beautiful white and black speckled coat. She was a bit overweight and quiet - and a little shy - which never made her a stand-out to potential adopters....But we spent hours and days and months with her....We knew how special she was. She always was a joy to walk, and she always went right into her kennel, obediently and with love for us and all who fed and walked her. She was always patient and sweet - even after weeks and weeks of us showing her to people and singing her praises - and then returning to her kennel after she was passed over for a puppy or a little fluffy dog.

It was a mystery to us - really - why she was never adopted in the 5 months she was with us. A five-year old dog is not always the desire of those looking for a pet - but Chloe was special because she was just so GOOD!! We figured her weight was the issue - and thankfully - after her lengthy stay with us - with exercise and the right food - she was looking and feeling great. We took new pictures of her and tried to create some interest - and we began to be cautiously hopeful for Chloe.

One cool autumn evening I got a call from an older couple who had lost their 15 year old spaniel mix and they wanted a mature and sweet dog because they were ready to love another. Before I could suggest Chloe - the man said to me "Well....My wife has already fallen in love with Chloe - on the website!" I was thrilled....we agreed to meet right away - and we did just that....I took along my best friend and devoted volunteer Christine for prayers and moral support. As we sat in the parking lot and made ready to meet the nice people parked just a few parking spots away - we thoroughly put it in God's hands as we bowed our heads and Chris prayed "Dear God - Please make this the home for Chloe! She needs a home so very badly!"

A few minutes into the meeting - we knew that our prayers and God's will for Chloe had had put us all together - as the sweet older lady put her hands on Chloe's shoulders and said the magic words "Do you want to come home with me?" A few more minutes - and Chloe was getting into the back seat of their car - freshly hugged and kissed by her long-term caretakers....Chloe set off on her journey into her next life - A life of love and warmth and being the only canine child of a couple who desperately needed her....who had come for only her....never to be passed over again.

"But if we hope for what we do not see, we wait for it with patience."
Romans 8:25

"Once Upon a Time"

Once upon a time - there was a wonderful married couple who encountered their empty nest syndrome just as their beloved 11 year old Short-haired Pointer, Gretchen, passed away. Though they were wanting to be active & enjoy the carefree life without the commitment and responsibilities of children and a pet....they soon both ached for the lost companionship of a dog. They both wondered what to do....

If they got a dog – would the new dog be able to take the place of their beloved Gretchen? They had her for eleven years....Gretchen could easily go on their boat with them – go in the car anywhere - and travel with them to their daughter's place in Toledo. They were not sure if a new dog would be that adaptable to their lives right off the bat.

They also were struggling with the thought of even trying to "replace" Gretchen.... Like they could ever do that! Their hearts were broken when she died and they were afraid that getting a new dog right away would somehow, perhaps, diminish – or dishonor her memory...

So - they went a long time - both afraid to take that chance on canine LOVE. Trisha, Gretchen's human mom – called me sometimes – interested in a puppy that I would post on Facebook or on my website...."What about this one?" she would say....and she would sigh and then tell me "I really just don't know what to do...When the time comes – I guess I'll know..." She said she was truly and mostly worried about Paul, her husband...."He was really upset about Gretchen....and I just don't know how to even start that conversation with him...."

And then came the Mastiff puppies – who were part Mastiff and part American Bulldog….Trisha saw the pictures on line and was immediately drawn to them…..ALL!!! She started talking with her hubby about it and apparently they both had a break down talking about how much they both missed having a dog…how much they missed Gretchen….and how afraid they were to love again….and yet – Trisha knew this was the time…..She called me and told me "I think we are ready – there is just something telling me there is something special about these puppies …. And we want a girl….and these are all girls….so now what do I do?"

I prayed about it and also felt that these puppies just had to meet Trisha and Paul – so I told her – "Just let the puppies do the work."

The next day I dropped by – knowing they were both at home after church – and I entered their kitchen with an armload of girl mastiff mix pups…There were three girls – a brindle one, and fawn one, and a black and tan one…Trisha looked at me with a huge grin on her face…."Well, Paul…what do you think?" she said….Paul played with all of them, laughing at the ways they all jumped around and played….

"These puppies are really something!" He laughed and he took notice of the black and tan one that seemed to keep running between he and his wife…It was as if this one little girl puppy knew exactly what her mission in this kitchen was – and she ran between them as if to say "Pick me! Pick me! Because I pick you!!"

Paul laughed at her sweet little face and the attention she paid to them exclusively – unlike either of the other puppies who were more interested in the rug and beveled trim on the woodwork.

"You want to come to me or Mommy?" He said – lifting up the little black and tan one and placing it on Trisha's shoulders and looking at her with a knowing and tearful expression…Trisha looked over the doggy's soft little head and into the eyes of her husband.

"Did you say Mommy?" Trisha asked – and they both held the puppy together with tears falling and complete quiet between them for a moment….

"Well?" Trisha Asked Paul….."Well?" Paul asked Trisha….at which point – I picked up the remaining two puppy girls and whisked them out of the kitchen quietly and out the back door to the van…..I did not go back to Trisha and Paul's house for a few hours and gave them time to get acquainted with to the new little one that had just filled that uncertain longing in their broken hearts and the vacant space in their empty nest….

That was a few years ago….and I am glad to report that Sasha Grace has become not only the love of her people's life – but a very adept traveler, boater, and wonderfully polite guest when they visit their daughter….And on the rare occasions when Sasha cannot go along with Paul and Trisha on their travels….I get to keep her and board her at my home or at the rescue, where I am sure she tells the dogs there every chance she gets to be patient and wait – because she was also a rescue dog who filled a spot in an empty nest….once upon a time.

"Whatever you ask in my name, this I will do, that the Father may be glorified in the Son." John 14:13

"Hands and Feet"

Freddy called me on a Tuesday. He needed me to come and get his little terrier mix right away....He made it sound very urgent....Lots of times people make wanting to get rid of their dogs sound urgent....Yep – lots of times people just want their dogs gone yesterday....But there was something different in Freddy's tone.... When I spoke with him on the phone and he sounded very old - his breathing was stifled and he told me he'd had COPD and Lung Cancer. His voice was very shaky. He told me he had to find a home for his little dog because he was going into hospice soon and his prognosis was not good. "I probably won't be here much longer....I am just not able to look after the little guy." I told him I was so sorry and I would love to take his little dog.

I jumped into the van and an hour later, I was driving in some unknown trailer park in a town about an hour south. I was afraid when I found his lot number – because it looked so forlorn...almost abandoned. Trailer 457 was a run-down place on the outside - with a broken side door which I accidentally went to instead of the porch that was hidden by some little trees on the other side...The man who came to the side door pointed for me to go around. He did not look terribly old - but had oxygen on - which made me know I had the right place.

Once I entered the tiny dwelling – however - I was pleasantly surprised. It was very nice and bright - with just the right amount of clutter in it to make it warm and cozy. He obviously kept house as well as he could. There were all kinds of breathing machines and medical devices around the room - which made me sad - because Freddy - the owner of the trailer and the little dog (who came running to greet me) - was a 60-year-old small statured fellow with the prettiest blue eyes I'd seen a in while!! Freddie was not the old man he sounded to be on the phone – but a young-ish senior citizen - whose only apparent problem in life was breathing. Freddy's wife had passed in December with COPD and lung cancer too... She was only 56 and died the day after Christmas. He said they had both been suffering for two years. He told me "By the Grace of God - I was able to stay strong enough to take care of her. I prayed every day I would be well enough so she would not die alone," he said. Then he told me that in early January his health deteriorated.

He said, "I knew it would...but I can't really live without her - so it is probably a good thing. This is her dog - I got it for her in the fall when she got really bad and couldn't get up any more. He hasn't been the same since, either. I just want to find him a good home with people who will love him like we did"

He had all of "Mokie's" toys and bowls ready. All of his vet papers...He even had shampoo and conditioner for him. "You said you were a groomer - so I threw those in, too."

As I put all of Mokies things in the van –I realized that with each armload I was taking pieces of this man's life with me....He would be in hospice soon – and his life would soon be over....As much as I dreaded it – the last thing I had left to take out to the Van was Mokie....and it was time for him to say good bye.

I looked at him and his eyes were swimming in - I don't know - relief...remorse....grief? I did not know his story - if he had kids - or if he

74

had family - but I sensed he was feeling all alone at this moment. I told him I would keep in touch and then I grabbed his hand and just began praying. It seemed like the right thing to do. The words just came out - for his strength and his health and an easy passing into the arms of his Heavenly Father and his beautiful bride. Completely embraced by the love and power of God - we also hugged a long loving and powerful hug. He kissed little Mokie and told him to be good. Then He looked at me and told me I was an angel. "I really believe you were sent by God." He said, wiping his eyes.

Now, I am certainly not sure about the angel part - but I really believe I had been sent there on some kind of a Divine Appointment, for sure! Thank you, God for sending us out and putting us in places where we can truly be your hands and feet - and even rescue for little dogs - when need be. Amen!

"But for this very purpose have I let you live, that I might show you My power, and that My name may be declared throughout all the earth." Exodus 9:16

"The 'JOY' of Rescue"

Joy had been at Here Doggie Doggie rescue since June 22. She was a dump-off ...Abandoned on a back county road - and she came to us with a bounce in her step and - apparently - just happy to be alive!! We named her "Joy" - because of the look on her face....because of the spring in her gait and the enthusiasm with which she always embraced each day. Outside in the play yard - she would run around with the other dogs - smiling and throwing her head back over her shoulders as if she had just pulled off some kind of a practical joke.

After three months in the rescue - even dogs who are appropriately named "Joy" would get impatient and discouraged - one would imagine....But Joy never seemed to become institutionalized - as some dogs who are held long-term eventually do. She was always appreciative of her food, receptive of any attention, and able to entertain herself by playing with her neighbors and lounging in the sun when she was turned outside.

Once in a while, though, I would see her head against her cage in the evenings - after supper - when everyone was going off to sleep. Her big brown eyes would look around the rescue room and her head would droop a little, and she would sigh. I knew she longed for a home...but it was as if she was hiding her dreams from us behind her happy personae day after day. We all loved Joy so much....and we knew that she was waiting for that moment when she would get a forever home - I think we all wished for Joy to get her turn.

Thankfully, Her day came on the last day of our Here Doggie Doggie Rummage Sale Fund Raiser - the end of the day on a Saturday....A sweet young mom and her three kids came into the shop asking about a dog that would be a good fit for their grandma - "Not too old - but a good size for protection. Something pretty easy for her to handle." We immediately thought of Joy.....We brought her out and after her initial greeting - which was met with enthusiasm - she settled right down and began leaning on the family....She stood beside them and let the kids all touch her - and she was patient and loving with them....showing the true wonders of her personality.

The family decided to go and get the grandma so she wouldn't miss out on this opportunity to adopt such a wonderful dog....Even though we all knew at the shelter that she had been there a really long time and she probably wasn't going anywhere soon....

In a short while - Grandma and the family returned. Joy was even more wonderful with the grandmother - going to the door and asking to go out when she had to go and do her business - demonstrating just how very housebroken she was. The grandmother was actually someone I knew as a grandmother to one of my son's good friends - and I assured her that she would have very few problems with Joy. Again Joy stood beside them and it was easy to see that she was comfortable just existing with them, and standing among them as they talked about her.

Then the grandmother said the magical words "Do you want to come home with me?" to Joy...and that was all it took. Joy's nose - from then on - was planted by the front door. Joy was smart enough to know what those words meant...She had seen dog after dog after puppy have those words spoken to them, and she knew that her moment had arrived. She was getting a forever home with grandma!! She would have kids to play with and a family of her own to love....And she was so ready!!!

It is a funny thing - some less enlightened people really think that animals have no feelings or cannot show appreciation or emotion....but after the paperwork was signed and Joy's adoption was a done deal - Joy pulled herself from the front door and walked to each of the Here Doggie Doggie staff and volunteers and kissed our hands or our cheeks goodbye as if to say "Thank you for taking me in and finding me a home. Thank you for caring for me all of this time."

And then as soon as the front door was opened - she bounded into the family minivan with so much - well....JOY - that the weeks and months she spent longing for a new home seemed to vanish behind her with each step. Joy was in her family's car - with her new family....and no doubt planning her first practical joke on them so that they, like us, could experience so much JOY!!!

"May the God of hope fill you with all joy and peace in believing, so that by the power of the Holy Spirit you may abound in hope." Romans 15:13

"Keep on Truckin'"

"I liked him immediately" my assistant Krys said to me about the very big man who was sitting in a chair at the table in the grooming and rescue shop with a peek-a-poo in his lap. I was out of the shop for a moment - and when I walked in the door - I found this large and talkative fellow sitting at the table - talking to Krys and the other volunteers who were there for the day....Frank - a truck driver from Louisiana had just parked his 18-wheeler in front of the shop and walked in the door and said "I want a dog who will travel with me." Krys had him sit down at the table and instinctively released two of our sweetest little dogs for him to meet....and as usual - one of them picked him before he ever had the chance to look at either of them. Cocoa the Peek-a-poo turned the corner from the back room where she had been napping and jumped right into his arms and began kissing his chin.....

This is where I came in...Frank's large hands were cupping the little dog's face and he was looking into her huge and happy eyes. "You wanna go in the big truck with me?" he asked.... I don't know if it was her enthusiastic tail wags or her adorable face - but this big and apparently lonely trucker had tears in his eyes that I couldn't ignore. "Oh - look at you, are those tears of joy?" I asked him and he smiled sideways at me with a big grin and said "No - I'm allergic to dogs!" And then he laughed a laugh that was every bit as big as he was, as he wiped his eyes.

While Krys was filling out his adoption paperwork and we were all sitting around visiting with this sweet traveler - he told us that he passes by here a few times a week - but actually lives in Louisiana. "I load out of Mineral City - and have passed here a lot in the past month thinking I should just see if you adopt out dogs here. I decided today I'd take a chance." - he told us - petting little cocoa's head the entire time he spoke. He went on to tell us about his other dog at home who he shares with his neighbors, and he told us stories about all of his other dogs he has owned and lost. We knew for sure that Cocoa was going to be a spoiled little gypsy - riding with this tender-hearted dog lover.

"She's gonna go in the truck with me.. I need a riding companion. I hope she likes the truck...."

It did not take us long to find out. In a few minutes - he was loading her in the truck. Krys and I watched from the front door of the shop while he talked to her and pointed out everything in the truck to her. Then he climbed in and sat in the driver's seat. Cocoa peeked her little head out from under his seat and looked at us as if to say good bye as he shut the door.

Moments later - Cocoa and Frank were motoring north on Rt. 800....Krys said to me "That is the first time we have ever watched a dog drive away IN her new home!" and I laughed about that. I walked back in the shop - but Krys watched until they were out of sight - and then told me that they had disappeared into their new life. I smiled - thinking about how blessed we both were to have the opportunity to see this happy union occur...I thought about the shop - and how much I loved it that at this new location along this stretch of road - we were at just the right place for Frank to Find us - and for Cocoa to Find him....and I said a little prayer - asking God to Bless them with safe travels and sweet adventures on the road - together in the big truck.

"The heart of man plans his way, but the Lord establishes his steps."
Proverbs 16:9

"The Language of Love"

He came into the rescue on a Saturday...and he was terrified. His eyes were wider than any dog I have ever rescued before....and his actions were very strange. He would walk a few steps and then sit down....He looked around with a wild look in his eyes.....When we spoke to him, he would tilt his head and literally look right into our faces with not a spark of familiarity in what we were saying....We struggled to understand his sketchy ways and his sudden fright at just about any loud noise....

And then – eventually - it dawned upon us.....Bombi - a Border Terrier Mix – had been picked up in a Spanish speaking community....in a Mexican mobile home park that was probably inhabited by migrant workers throughout the summer. He did not understand what we were saying and was completely out of his element because he did not understand our language....Bombi did not "speak" English.

Bombi - as far as we can figure – had been named from some form of the Latin word Bambino - meaning baby. At only six months old - he literally was a baby....but the family who had originally owned Bombi treated him like anything but a baby....He had been tied to a tree and pretty much kicked or ignored or yelled at by everyone in his household. My assistant Krys had been contacted by her mom who alerted us to the situation. She'd tried desperately to get him rescued - and after an interpreter spoke with the family - they willingly surrendered Bombi to us to find him a suitable home.

So poor Bombi came to us - a little on the thin side, with abuse in his background and with the additional challenge of a language barrier -

something we did not know much about.....We figured if we exposed him to us as much as possible – maybe he would get that not all people were like the people in the trailer park.

So one day - while Krys and I were there cleaning, we let him out to run around with us while we cleaned the shop so that he could get away from the chaos of the rescue room and learn that he could trust us. We plied him with doggie treats and as much contact from us as he could stand....Suddenly we heard a scratching noise and discovered Bombi playing with a piece of tape that was stuck on an old box stacked by the trash by the back door....We realized that Bombi our little Spanish baby wanted to play!! So that gave us an idea....

We grabbed a tennis ball and started throwing it against the floor and the walls to make it bounce. Bombi instinctively chased it and eventually figured out how to pick it up and chew on it. We began playing with him, and he seemed delighted by the sudden attention and praise. Even if he could not understand what we were saying to him - he could figure out that we were just happy to see him happy....and that our gentle pats on the head and our nuzzles of encouragement were meant to make him happy.

That day, as his fear of us lessened somewhat - he walked over to Krys, and put his head on her lap. Gently, she stroked his fuzzy little chin and he climbed up on her lap and snuggled close to her. Some of the wildness had left his eyes and he looked less concerned and frightened. As she held him and he relaxed some more - I realized that this might be a first for him....the first time he had been held....the first time he had been encouraged and played with....and the first time that the affection that is inherently born in a dog was ever returned to him.

"He understands that" I said to Krys - as she looked up at me with the knowing grin that rescuers get when they realize that they have made a connection - and that the connection is about to make a difference.

For as rescuers - we know too well the fear of those who have been mistreated....we know the sketchy looks and the confusion and learned helplessness of all living things that have been so powerless. A language barrier presented a new challenge to us for only a moment - until we decided to speak and act and minister to this pup in a way that conveyed the universal language of love....And the change that it brings...and the feeling it creates - truly needs no words.

"And the Lord said, "Behold, they are one people, and they have all one language, and this is only the beginning of what they will do. And nothing that they propose to do will now be impossible for them." Genesis 11:6

"Love is Patient"

"Fang gets to sleep in a bed tonight!" my loyal volunteer and
BFF Christine said to me as we cleaned up the day's pooh and food dishes.
It had been a long time since Fang had slept in anything other than a
cage....After all he had been there since June!!! But Fang had waited
patiently for his adoption day to come....

Fang always had a plucky personality....He's just kinda always rolled with
the punches....He never minded getting moved from smaller cages to
bigger cages and back to small cages to sleep in as our population
dictated....and he stood perfectly still when I shaved him down for his first
grooming AND second grooming while in our care!! And even after he
was passed over...time after time...he kept his chin up and kept positively
playful and sweet to every volunteer and prospective adopter he ever met.

A few weeks ago - he worked his charm on an adopter who came in with
her three grandchildren to pick out a family pet. The grand-daughter fell in
love with Fang - but the older Grandson fell in love with Queenie - a
shepherd mix with a soft coat and gentle brown eyes who also had no
apparent faults....The youngest grandson - really didn't care that much as
long as he got kisses from both.....No matter how long the little family
went back and forth - listing the pros and cons of each dog - it came right
down to the boy loving Queenie more - and the grand-daughter loving her
brother more than her own choice....After a brief pow-wow and the little
girl saying "I just want a dog, I guess - it really doesn't matter to me....."
the family went with Queenie - The little boy just loved Queenie - and his
sister unselfishly let his choice come before hers.

As we filled out the paper work for Queenie and put Fang back in his cage - there was this feeling of bitter-sweetness to the whole ordeal....We knew that Fang had loved that little girl - as much as Queenie loved the little boy - and since the grandma said they only had room for one dog - we felt terrible about Fang - and at the same time - so happy for Queenie..... Well - as God would have it - the end of the story had not yet been written for Fang...

Earlier this week - I got an email and then a phone call from Maryanne - the grandmother of the children who had picked Queenie..."We just keep thinking about him, and I really think that Queenie might do better adjusting to life outside of the rescue if she had a housemate and companion....." Maryanne said.....

My heart jumped when I heard her take a long pause on the other end of the phone...."Can I come and get Fang on Monday?" She asked me......I smiled and said "Of course!!" and then - hanging up the phone - happy tears welled up as I realized that Fang would get his little girl and she would get him.....

Maryanne came in on Monday afternoon and this time she came in alone.

"Sidney has just been so wonderful in helping out with Queenie - and she talks about Fang all the time - but plays with Queenie, too.....I just wanted to surprise her...." So Fang was groomed once more before he left - spritzed with doggy cologne and looking dapper with his first hours in the company of his sweet little girl .....

"Can you imagine?" Chris said to me turning around from the sink later that night as we put all of the day's schmutz in its place and talked over the events of the day "Can you just imagine that little girl coming home from school today and finding Fang there - waiting for her?"

We both got teary eyed thinking about the happy reunion and the forever bond they would share now - finally being able to be together......"Ahhhhh" - said Chris wiping her eyes...."And he gets to sleep in a bed tonight!! A BED!!!" it had been a long time coming for Fang - but God's timing is always perfect - and Fang's new forever home was definitely worth the wait!!

"But if we hope for what we do not see, we wait for it with patience."
Romans 8:25

"Comfort and Hope"

They were all looking at me. Big beautiful eyes - Round and Hopeful. Waiting and pleading at me while I "Shopped". It was - at one moment - the most joyful experience I have ever felt as a dog rescuer addicted to the adrenaline rush of being in the company of 60 dogs who needed rescued.....and at the same time - the most desperate feeling in the world knowing that I could only take a portion of them all. I walked "the lines"...the rows of cages - looking at them - looking into their hopeful eyes....stopping to love on each one and see how they would respond. There weren't any who growled at me......there weren't any who I would deem "unworthy" of being rescued.....so my task was a tough one.

Choosing someone else's fate has never been my job - so I prayed to God to help me make my choices well....
I saw gorgeous dogs. Big dogs with beautiful coats, and friendly hounds who lingered at their cage door after I passed by - then jumped readily - showing me their best stuff - as I walked by again. I saw terrified babies.....shaking by their doors - but offering my hand a kiss and making direct eye contact with me between shivers - hoping that they would be chosen. Some of them were....Some of them I had to leave behind....I tried to pick what hit my heart and also what I knew would fit in the van and would help Lawrence County Pound empty their cages and make room for more babies to come in.

They get so many every day!!

But when it was all said and done - 20 lives were saved from the Lawrence County Pound yesterday....and three from Pike county - just up the road about an hour.....
On the way back - Barbara - the wonderful lady from Rescue Me Ohio who rented the van and drove us both down sat in the passenger seat next

to me as I took my turn to drive the 4 hours back home from these high-kill shelters. Barb was looking at her phone and she said "Oh my - Lawrence is posting New dogs that came in already today - and there are lots of them!!" I felt bad - because this meant that some of the babies I had just seen might be on their way to being euthanized already.....and I wondered if I even made a dent in the real problem that faces these terribly rural pounds daily....Too many dogs - too many not spade or neutered....too many to make a difference.....

Once we had gotten home and I was busy with the business of washing the filth of a long terrifying drive off of 20 dogs - I smiled as each of them let me scrub them and they began to relax....I wrapped them each in a towel and put them in a clean warm spot with water and food and big, long hugs. The knowledge that they would not be harmed or euthanized - or made to feel afraid that they might not make it to another day made me smile. Knowing that the problem that exists in these same shelters – and in way too many other shelters made me very sad....and I tried to take my mind off of the pleading eyes and the fact that I just could not save every one I'd walked by, and I focused on the 20 warm bodies that lay happy and clean in the new small and cozy room that had been created by my assistant Krys and all of the wonderful volunteers who showed up just for them at the rescue that day....and I knew....We might not have been able to save them all - but for the 20 that were warm and safe - we made a real difference.....
And again I looked into their eyes - their sweet, living, innocent faces - and they looked back.....their big beautiful eyes - round and hopeful.

"And now, O Lord, for what do I wait? My hope is in you." Psalm 39:7

"For Crying out Loud!"

Tonight I had 2 dogs barking and crying in the rescue room....One was Checkers - the last puppy from a litter of Boxer-Beagle puppies that was rescued a while back.... Checker's brother Stubby was adopted today and tonight is his first night ever -all alone...The other crying dog in the rescue room was Bon-Bon - a Yorkie pup that was just rescued today. I can only be certain that he was crying because he missed his family, and was in an unfamiliar place surrounded by smells and sounds and even light that was completely unfamiliar....

These puppies were only a few feet apart in separate pens - they were within sight of one another I thought maybe putting them at eye level with each other might help them both feel a kinship...I thought maybe they would even be able to play with each other through the pens – like so many of the other dogs in the rescue do....But instead – they were both just still crying!!

So - I tried playing music for them on the radio...I tried leaving the light on for them...and I tried turning on a fan for some white noise. Nothing seemed to relieve their grieving. Each new variable I added into the equation seemed to make matters worse – and their crying became more intense...

Finally - I decided to let them bunk together in a huge cage that Checkers once shared with his siblings. The worst that could happen, I thought, is that they would not like each other and they would go back to their crying and barking in separate cages.....Nothing could be any worse than it already was with both of them crying!!

I put the two babies in the cage together – and a marvelous thing happened.....The rescue room fell silent...The two pups curled up together in the back of the cage.....and went to sleep...

I don't know if it is because misery loves company....or because they could totally relate to each other...but I imagine that it is the same for animals as it is for human beings when faced with loss, and grief, and loneliness. Sometimes - the best medicine is just being able to share these emotions with someone who gets the emptiness in your soul and the sadness in your heart....someone who will just hold you and say "I understand".

"Let brotherly love continue." Hebrews 13:1

"Rescued, by God"

One night, I showed Sally – a sweet dog that was rescued from the Harrison County Animal Shelter - to a lady who thought she was interested in her. She took one look at this precious baby and said "OH - I just don't think she is going to work out for me at all"......She took no time with her - never got down on the ground so that Sally could show her what a great dog she was. I watched as she literally pushed her away....she said "I am looking for more of a schnauzer....She is a little too skinny."...... I wanted to say "Sally can hear you!!"

I mean - I understand that people want what they want - and if there is no attraction there - I get it.....But this dog was just precious – standing there waiting to be noticed and loved!!! This dog needed a home - and she just wanted to please and a chance to show the very best of herself...
As I drove her home, tears rolled down my face. I felt worse than if I had been pushed away myself.

Truth is - I could really identify with this little girl. She was not perfect. She'd had a few pups and her body had changed from the young firm pup that she once was.....She was a bit too skinny...and a little clumsy ....BUT her heart was huge and all she wanted to do is give it to someone.

And that – possibly – just summed up the last 30 years of my life.

Those moments of rejection for the rescue dogs often puts me in a funk...Truth is - I feel like a rescued dog a lot of the time - and not just because I share the rent with so many other rescues. We really do have so much in common.

Sometimes I wonder - what exactly was I rescued for? Sometimes I feel displaced and rejected - by life - by friends. By people I desperately want to accept me just the way I am - but because of agendas and conflicts in our different convictions they find just the flaws and not the inner beauty....

And then I remember my tears for this little one....and as always - I go to my Father. I just have to remember that God has a plan for all of us. We all have a permanent home with Him - and that He has placed us in the world where He knows we might not always be accepted - but we will be forged into the person He has intended us to be....And just as it breaks His heart to see us rejected and pushed away....His own son endured this for all of us so that at the end of our journey - we will not ever be pushed away or "Homeless" again. My Lord is the ultimate rescue. Always!!

And - as for Sally, the dog - I had my prayers for her as well. The same prayer I have for all of the dogs. I know I would rather see Sally – and all of them - wait for the right person...than to settle for someone who cannot see how incredible each and every one of them is - flaws and all. God has that person in mind for every dog in the rescue if we just wait long enough....and he has that right person in mind for all of us as well.

"For my father and my mother have forsaken me, but the Lord will take me in." Psalm 27:10

"Seeing is believing"

This weekend, I groomed a blind yellow lab named Jake. I have known Jake and his owner Laurie for several years. They were the willing recipients of my services during my newspaper delivery years...and Jake used to come over to the car and sniff and lick my hands when he could still make out shadows. Jake has a retinal disease that causes the lenses to cloud and turn a very pretty shade of iridescent green at its onset - and eventually cloud over completely. He is about 12 years old now - and had good vision until he was about 7 or 8 years old....then his sight began to diminish. He now has two cold green stones where his beautiful eyes used to look with expression.

Jake is amazing. I watched him in my shop - which was completely foreign to him - navigate the walls, the floor, and my equipment while he sniffed and made his way around the place. He walked with great care - and really used his body, and his ears and nose to help him along this completely uncharted territory. A few times he walked into a wall or put his nose in a door - but he always just regrouped and tried again. I watched him, thinking how many things a human could learn - just from watching Jake.

First of all, Jake had once had his sight. His blindness came later in life and he had to accept this "disability". However, he did not give up and lay down and let his people wait on him. He learned how to re-invent his existence - relying on his other senses and instinct to survive. Second, Jake allows himself to fail. He accepts that as just part of his deal. He walks into walls, he falls down, he bumps into things. But he never gives up. He doesn't sit in the middle of a grooming shop crowded with equipment and new smells and cry. He just "sees" it as a new challenge. I have had sighted dogs act much worse their first time in my shop. But Jake calmly plods along....bumps and bruises - no doubt - but willing to take the hit and find his way. Thirdly - Jake proceeds with CAUTION. He does not just charge forward. He uses his head. He goes cautiously into new situations.....Walking by faith - if you will - and not by sight....because he cannot see.

Watching Jake - I realized that he probably experienced more of my grooming shop than most dogs that visit....heck - even me sometimes - by cautiously examining each piece of hair on the floor....each corner and smell as he felt everything along the way.

Finally - I must credit Laurie with the amazing parenting that she has done with Jake. She has allowed him to grow into his new role by letting him fail. That to me would be so difficult as a doggie mom to watch. But it is obvious that her pain in allowing this has paid off in Jake. She has guided him and encouraged him - but she has let him do the work - which has made him "Abled" and not "Disabled".

By the time I got done with Jake on Saturday - I felt that he really knew me - and I felt Honored to know him. Sitting with him on the floor and feeling him lean into the massage and the warm air from the dryer - I knew that he was living in the moment - not distracted by anything. I envied his experience of the world for a bit - realizing that he actually knew so much about his world - by "seeing" with his instinct and having to learn to walk completely by faith. So strange to be taught so much in one day by a blind dog - and realize that as humans - we still have so much to learn.

"For we walk by faith, not by sight." II Corinthians 5:7

"What's in a Name?"

Dexter came to me a few weeks ago. He came from a man who had obviously house-trained him well - but could not keep him because he just would let him out to run around - and the man kept getting calls from his neighbors to keep the dog in his yard.... He surrendered him so that he could find a better home with people who could spend more time with him and take better care of him.

Dexter is a white boxer with patches of Red Brindle and when he stands beside my brindle boxer Ruby - he looks like they are twins - except he is wearing Charlie Brown's Ghost costume with the holes cut out in the sheet all over. He is gentle and sweet and amazingly well-mannered for a boxer.

I was working with him for about a week - when my old friend Becky Bowman asked me in a message on Facebook if I knew of any boxers because they had been looking for one. I told her about Dexter and she came to see him the next day!!

She fell in love - Then she told me the rest of the story.

Her oldest boy, Brock, had been bitten once by a dog and was very apprehensive towards all strange dogs - big or small. "I know that Boxers are great with kids and thought that might be a good place to start!" she said. "It will really be up to the boys - I will want them to meet him here - and see how they act together. I don't want him to be afraid."

So a few days later - the boys came over. I had everyone sit on the floor (my dog-hair-filled wooden floor) and Dexter sniffed and walked around like a prince to meet everyone. He seemed to sense Brock's fear and shyness – so he focused mostly on the younger boy, Jack. Dexter would play with Jack – who was immediately smitten – but he circled around Brock - waiting for an invitation.

"Here – hold out your hand, "Becky coaxed Brock. Dexter's neck extended just as far as it possibly could towards Brock's hand, and gently – Dexter licked his fingertips with the very end of his tongue…Dexter was very cautious to not scare Brock – and in a few minutes they were getting along very well – and moving closer towards each other as the minutes of this meet and greet passed….Once they all got to know each other - it became a dog and 3-person love affair on my hairy wooden floor. The boys were already thinking of a middle name for him - and they came up with some good ones!!

The boys interacted so well with Dexter - and Dexter - in turn - was a gentleman...He was playful and silly - and he showed all his sides to the family so that they knew exactly what they would be getting into. The boys asked me really good questions about training and growing...and keeping him in the yard. Becky had done her homework on finding just the right dog for her kids…and I was amazed at how she left it completely up to them – even though I knew she loved Dexter already – so much!!

Becky and the boys made arrangements to pick up Dexter the very next day and they all went out with plans of going to the pets store to get Dexter all of his new toys and a leash and a collar with a tag for his name…..Going out the door – the boys were still talking middle names reciting them all - sandwiched between "Dexter" and "Bowman"…..

When the boys got into the truck and Becky and I were still inside….Dexter sat down right in front of the door, gave a quick "Yelp." and looked down - like "Where did they go without me?"

Becky patted his head and smiled at me with a knowing and thankful grin….

"Don't worry Dexter - You'll be a full-fledged Bowman tomorrow afternoon!!" Becky told him.

And I think as far Dexter was concerned – in his heart he had already become a full-fledged Bowman - no matter what middle-name he'd end up with!!!

"A good name is to be chosen rather than great riches, and favor is better than silver or gold." Proverbs 22:1

"Timing is Everything!"

They came in the shop late in the afternoon - as fate would have it. This nice young woman and her sister and their children...I remembered them - because it had only been a few weeks since one of them had adopted an adult dog from us and returned it because it had been too rambunctious for her toddler - and they had decided to get a puppy next time we got any puppies into the rescue. The young woman had felt so awful for the failed adoption - so bad - in fact - she had her husband return the dog with a long explanation about why it did not work out.

I understood.....I always consider that the adoptions - successful or unsuccessful - are God's will. The volunteers and I pray for the dogs when they come in - for God to find them the perfect forever home....and then trust that He will work on the situation. We can only provide the space, the time, and the advertisement!

So - as fate would have it - these young ladies came into the shop. We were done - for the most part - for the day. And I was planning on going to dinner...but as I always say - We plan - and God laughs!!

The one young woman came in and fell in love with the Norwegian Elkhound-Lab/hound puppies. "I should really wait until my husband is here - but he works in the oilfield and has weird hours!" She said...."But I am going to go call him and if he agrees - we will be back!" I could tell she was just so excited. "How late will you be here?" She asked....I told her I was hoping to be done by 5 - but I never knew for sure.....

Well - 5 o'clock came with a flurry of visitors in the rescue....First a nice man brought in his collie to make an appointment...then a friend stopped to visit and we talked for quite a while....My best friend's son stopped by to hang some new lights in the rescue room....and my daughter visited, too....and just as we were completely out of the shop - lights out - front door locked - in our cars...the young women came pulling in slowly beside me. I waved excitedly at them and we got out of our cars laughing.

"Does this mean a puppy gets to go home?" I asked.....The young woman looked embarrassed "My hubby agreed - and I was afraid you'd be gone - but my sister said - 'Well take a chance and go down - and if God wants you to have this puppy tonight, they will still be there!'"

I raised my hand toward heaven and said "YES!!!" and we all went back into the rescue.....As fate would have it - a sweet male puppy picked her out by rubbing his little nose into her shoulder the minute she held him. As fate would have it - that puppy was cradled on the sisters front lap as the very excited and happy woman hugged me and thanked me for still being there....."God's will obviously!" I said ....She giggled "Obviously!!" As fate would have it - that puppy gets to sleep in a bed with his new family - and that family's quest for a new dog ends with many twists and turns and keenly orchestrated timing - As God would have it!!

"For still the vision awaits its appointed time; it hastens to the end—it will not lie. If it seems slow, wait for it; it will surely come; it will not delay." Habakkuk 2:3

"Landing in the Lap of Open Hearts"

Christine and I got the impression that the man in front of us was a rescue as well....He met us in Akron with his two "Spiritual Friends" as he called them.....and we kind of got the impression that he had a "Foster Family" of his own.....Howard called me several days ago at the rescue and asked me if I had any little dogs he could adopt...."I am in the place right now where I am lonely for a companion and can have a dog - and I think a dog would be the best kind of companion I could imagine," he'd said.

I could tell by talking with him that he was an older African-American Gentleman - probably in his late sixties to early seventies....He was quick with a laugh and wanted to talk about his choice of a dog at length as I told him about all the little lap dogs we had at the rescue...."I believe one of the little chi-weenies sounds like it could be the one and I was hoping for a girl...but bring a few so I can choose. We got a big pretty fenced in yard and a really nice house," he said proudly - and we agreed to meet at 2:30 on Saturday....

The first thing I noticed about Howard when I met him was his Veteran Army hat with several decorations on it - signifying awards of honor....I did not know what they meant - not that it mattered - but I shook his hand and thanked him for his service promptly - as my father had often taught me to do with Veterans of any branch of armed services....The second thing I noticed about Howard was that he was flanked on either side by middle aged white folks - A couple whose names were Todd and Cheryl..."My Spiritual Friends" he called them....As we began to show Howard the four chi-weenies we brought for him to choose from - they joined him in his delight at each one....They were very helpful in him holding the two that he wanted to see and were so pleased when he chose one that would be getting into the car and going home with them.....

As the choice was being made - I turned to Cheryl and asked her - "Are you folks in the market for a doggie too?" and she smiled and said "No" And then added "Well - obviously we are - I mean - Howard is getting one...." and it began to dawn on me the relationship between Howard and his "Spiritual Friends".

I had read somewhere about a program where people take Veterans into their homes to live as family when they have nowhere else to go...It is sponsored through the V.A. and it is very much akin to the work that we do at our shelter...People open their hearts and homes to someone who still has much life to live and much love to give - and both parties are the better for it.....and we certainly got the impression from Todd and Cheryl...AND Howard that this was the relationship and the circumstances in this case...

What is even more awesome is that Howard chose Britney - one of the five chi-weenies who had been brought by the homeless man - and whose former neighbor threatened to shoot all of them if we did not take them in....Britney had been at the shelter for several months and we had been praying that she would find a soft place to land...Obviously God had been working overtime on this one - because not only did she find that soft place - but she'd found it in the lap of someone who had also been taken in and loved - and now they would both live in the 'really nice house' and 'big pretty fenced in yard' of his "Spiritual Friends" who had once again opened their home and their hearts with love.

"Little children, let us not love in word or talk but in deed and in truth." 1 John 3:18

"Shedding Off the Past"

Caroline is a husky-shepherd mix who was found walking down I-77 in
North Carolina by a girl who was on her way to visit her Grandmother in
Carrollton, Ohio – right around the corner from us. When the girl pulled
off the highway and got Caroline into her car - she went to the nearest exit
and called the local Dog Warden in the area and talked to him about the
dog she had just rescued from the side of the road. The Warden said there
were no reports of a dog missing that fit that description, and that they
normally just destroy dogs who are found on the highway because they are
most likely drop-offs from people passing through. Since they do not
know that much about them - they usually just come out and put them
down, and that he would be out to do just that. The girl refused to let that
happen, and she put Caroline back in her car and brought her all the way
to Carrollton to her grandmother's house.

The Grandma called me last week to tell me about this dog and asked if
we could take her in. Of course......we said.....of course!!

Krys - my rescue assistant at the time - named her Caroline - since she
had come to us from the Carolinas....and Krys and I both began trying to
bring poor Caroline out of her shell. Mostly she sat in the back of her cage
and when she went outside, she preferred to go to the furthest point of the
yard all alone. She was terrified. Our attempts to make her feel welcome
and loved were met with mostly stares and very little interaction. Her
behavior was a bit sketchy and we were never sure if she was going to lick
us or bite us - because she always seemed capable of both. Caroline was
also dirty!! We did not know how long she had been on the run - but her
white fur was dingy and she had started to blow out her winter coat. It
hung in big dirty whisps on her and she looked like Pigpen from the
Peanuts gang when she walked - stuff just kind of fell off all around her.

Yesterday I decided to give Caroline a bath. I didn't care if she wanted to be handled or not. It was hot and she needed a good scrubbing. The Groomer in me longed to brush out the rest of her coat and get her at least looking - if not - feeling - better. She did not like it. She fought me through most of the whole bath and when she was finally rinsed - ran out the back door and shook the grime of being lost and lonely and apparently feeling unloved off of her dripping fur - because after she had run around the back yard and taken the time to let the sun begin to air-dry her fur....she became for us - a different dog.

When I sat down to brush her out - she came right over to me and put her head under my hand the way dogs do when they want to be touched....I began brushing away the remains of her former life and she snuggled closer and closer - as if to say "Hurry up and make me pretty! I have a new life to live." I can honestly say that I have never seen a dog personify the word "Shed" the way that Caroline did......Yes - her hair was blown out like most dogs - but as each old tuft hit the ground- it was as if she was being reborn......She looked younger, more at peace, and I think she finally felt something she probably had not felt in a very long time - if ever.......She felt Loved.
It is amazing what love can do.....It can change circumstances....it can keep people alive.....it can give us all hope. And it can even make an old abandoned dog believe that it can be beautiful, and worthy of a bath, a brushing, and perhaps - someday - a new home and family. I am hopeful for Caroline - because she has finally turned a corner ....She has learned that it is safe to feel Love again - and return that love without fear of ever being lost or abandoned again.

"And I will give them one heart, and a new spirit I will put within them. I will remove the heart of stone from their flesh and give them a heart of flesh." Ezekiel 11:19

"Divine Appointment with a Beagle"

Yesterday was one of those days when I find myself in awe of the things that God has plotted out and planned for me - before the sun even rises - or I take my first conscious breath. Two days ago - I spoke to Rose about adopting a Beagle. She had called because she had seen one of my ads and was very taken with Beagley - an 11 month old Beagle who is sweet and loving. She told me that her old dog of 20 years had recently passed away - and she was sure that her other dog would surely die of a broken heart because she was not eating and she was in mourning over the other dog dying. She then asked me if I could hold Beagley until July - because she is on disability and would not be able to pay the $55 adoption fee for Beagley until then. I told her I would rather have her take Beagley right away and pay me when she gets paid due to her own dog suffering so much, and she was very thankful.

As we talked - she disclosed to me that she was disabled...when we were trying to arrange a time for us to meet for her to pick up the dog - she was hesitant - telling me she had to be home because she was in the process of getting a hospital bed installed in her living room. When I asked her who it was for she said "Well......me." I was floored - here this woman finally told me she had Liver Disease, Lung Disease and Diabetes - and she was worried about the suffering of her own little dog. I couldn't stand it. I opened up my mouth and the words just came out ...."Rose - You do not have to pay a penny for Beagley....and I will bring her to you." Rose immediately started to cry - and even called me back 10 minutes after we had made arrangements for me to come to bring the dog to her - just to make sure I was not kidding her. "Why would you do that?" she asked "Why would you do that for someone you don't even know?" I simply replied through my own tears "because it is the right thing to do...just chalk it up as a God thing." I told her. She said in a small sweet little voice "Ok, I will!"

Yesterday morning - with Beagley in a fresh cage - I drove to the Ellet area of Akron to find Roses' home to deliver Beagley. Rose lives in a little trailer park right off Canton Road and after driving around in a little bit of a circle - I found Rose's trailer - front door wide open - waiting for Beagley. I had taken one of my male friends with me - since I was unsure of where I was going and if it would be safe.....No need to worry Rose greeted us with open arms.....Her son - who had vowed to take care of Beagley after Rose passes also was there to meet us.

Beagley ran around the trailer for a few minutes sniffing and getting acquainted with the smells of Rose's living quarters while we explained a little about Beagley and how to make her feel safe and secure in her new home. Rose already had food and water in a dish on the floor - and when Beagley began eating and drinking we felt pretty sure that Beagley felt at home.

And after the initial hellos and food and niceties - Beagley felt comfortable enough to go to Rose. She jumped up on her lap and let Rose touch her - then hug her - then Squeeze her - Beagley's tail wagging the whole time. Roses tears of joy fell on little Beagley and Beagley answered back with kisses and lovins over Roses soft and welcoming shoulder. As we turned to leave and I hugged Rose - the overwhelming urge to pray with her overcame me...and I asked the question that is always hard to ask but once God takes over it becomes impossible not to be obedient to His prompting. "Will you let me pray with you?" I asked her....She never hesitated and I took her hands. Words just fell from my mouth without effort and I was completely in awe of God's anointing on this very divine

105

appointment. I do not even know for sure what I said - but when I finished - she was crying and I was hugging her with great force. My friend and I left her and Beagley and her son and her other little dog with waves and kisses and tail wags - and God's Grace and Mercy behind us.

Driving home - I was high - higher than any substance could ever in life get me....happier than any Christmas morning could make me. God had truly had His hand on this doggie adoption from the very beginning - in so many ways.
Beagley had actually been found on Rt. 542 by my friend's son one pre-spring morning....and had stayed with them for over a month before coming to the rescue. They brought her to me when I opened my shop and had room for her - but yet she had not been adopted and was still there when Rose fell in love with her on the website......

My dear friend who went with me yesterday is not a huge believer in the power of God - but was there to witness - first hand - how everything happens for a reason....How God always had a plan for all of us.....even little wayward doggies to bless sick lonely people and provide just the right moment for bringing God's healing and love to just the right place at the right time.

Hard to believe that God could pack such a wallop into the destiny of one stray little Beagle....but with God all things are possible and Dogs have always been the truest reflection of His unconditional Love for us....I am just never sure just what God has plotted out and planned before the sun comes up - but as long as I awake and take that first conscious breath - I know for certain that I will remain open to whatever he has for me - even if it comes in the form of a Beagle!!!

"For no prophecy was ever produced by the will of man, but men spoke from God as they were carried along by the Holy Spirit." 2Peter 1:21

"Tucker's Creek"

Tucker was Abby and Travis' first baby....He is a German Short-Haired Pointer mix with a little bit of Beagle thrown in for good measure. He became their baby while Travis was deployed in Afghanistan. Abby took Tucker to all of the obedience classes offered through Pet Smart and worked with him daily - making him quite a wonderful baby for her to have. The training and work she put into him helped her pass the time while her husband was serving our country in a very dangerous place....The love that they felt for Tucker came naturally. Tucker is an awesome dog...and though Abby rescued him as just a pup - he rescued them both during their time apart - giving Abby something to think about other than her hubby's deployment - and giving Travis peace of mind knowing that Abby was busy training Tucker and having someone to keep her company while he was away.

But as life will have it - another baby soon came along in their lives. Tucker was not so thrilled about the new baby that was walking and talking and taking up Abby and Travis' time. Tucker began acting out in jealousy against the new baby - and sadly, though they loved him so much, Abby and Travis knew that they had to do what was right and protect their human baby from their canine baby. Tucker had become growly and resentful and a little unpredictable around their little boy - and they did not want to wait until something bad happened. Abby called me and tearfully told me that they needed to bring Tucker to the rescue so that I could find him a new home.....so one evening in mid-April - they brought Tucker, his toys, his paperwork, and all of his favorite things to the rescue. With wet cheeks and sweet words they held him one more time and told him he was a good dog - and left their first baby behind - devastated but hopeful he would find a good home.

Tucker was at the shelter for about a month and a half. He was a good dog - but headstrong and ornery as most hounds can be....His time ticked away without much interest from anyone.....Unfortunately - even with him being fixed and housebroken - there is not a great demand for a 4 year old pointer - even with his stunning credentials and advanced obedience training....It takes a special kind of person to come looking for a hound dog.....And fortunately, Renee was that special person.

Out of the blue - Renee called one day. She immediately said "I want to meet the German Short-Haired Pointer that you have on your website." She said her family was just in love with the breed and she was retiring soon and was looking for just the right one. She really wanted one that was a few years older so she wouldn't have to put up with the puppy stage....so we arranged for her to come and meet Tucker.

Renee walked in with a few toys already under her arm and eyes wide and hopeful. She told me that she was retiring in July from AEP in Akron and was moving to West Virginia. "My family has a 200 year old farm house that I inherited....I knew this was coming and I planned my life accordingly so that I would be young enough to enjoy the land." I asked her how much land? She replied "Oh - over 190 acres at least....this boy will be allowed the entire run of it. It has a pond and woods, and fields - he will be able to just take off and hike with me into the sunset of our old age!" She laughed. She said the farm was in Elizabeth, West Virginia - and she was the last of the great-grandchildren who wanted it and would keep it in the family.

The whole time she was talking, Tucker was running around in front of her - not too close - but playing with the toys she had brought him and looking at her - inquisitively. He finally got close enough that she started to pet him and he relaxed a little and let her hold him and talk to him. I have done this for longer than a minute - and I can usually sense when a bond is beginning.....and this was the moment.

Renee looked up at me over his beautiful dark brown speckled fur and said to me..."Here is the really bizarre thing about this." She began..."I had to meet him to see if he could be the right dog. I want to just retire down in the country and have a dog by my side - sitting on the porch and running through the fields....So I prayed for the right dog." She paused...and then continued. "He is perfect....and his name is Tucker...." she smiled "The name of the lane that the farm house is on is called "Tucker's Creek...so this one was just meant to be my baby"

Tears filled my eyes and that joyful shiver of knowing God's hand was on the situation from the beginning traveled up my spine and to the top of my head - giving me chills. Renee looked at Tucker and said "I want to take you home right now - and tonight we'll drive down to the farmhouse on Tucker's Creek....You have your house on your very own Creek...did you know that??" Tucker just panted and smiled. Minutes later - Tucker was seated in the passenger seat of her truck and driving away towards his new life. The next day - I shared the picture below with Abby and Travis that was sent to me by Renee. It is Tucker - playing at the farmhouse and laying on his new big rug - in front of the fireplace at his new home - on Tucker's Creek.

"And when Christ, who is your life, is revealed to the whole world, you will share in all his glory." Colossians 3:4

"Trouble!"

I knew I was in trouble when I heard Mark's voice on the phone. Such a gentle and sweet voice telling me that his old dog Chuck has passed away. He recounted the history of Chuck - how he'd gotten him, how he'd loved him and how they'd been constant companions - clear up to two weeks ago when Chuck had gotten mysteriously sick...Then Mark's voice trailed off and I heard him blowing his nose on the other end of the line....and his sorrow and grief cut right through me. "I just want Chuck," He said "but since I can't have him - I need another good dog....A companion."

Mark told me about his life. Mark was a War veteran. His platoon had gone into Vietnam after the action - taking down the camps and trying to find the POWs who might still be somewhere in country. He told me about all the places that he'd lived back in the states - how a veteran sometimes just doesn't find his right footing after having been through so much...and how he'd pretty much retired into a secluded haven in Harrison County just to find peace in nature and away from people. He said he had 28 fenced acres for a dog to explore and run through - he just needed the right one. I knew I was in trouble because I already knew who would be the right dog for Mark...and as I listened with an open heart - I knew it would have to be Pete.

Pete, the English Setter - was bred to be a bird dog and a hunter. Though these were the qualities of his particular breed - Pete was as gentle as a lamb - and was not at all interested in hunting. Unfortunately - his owner did not think that his gentle nature was an asset and he beat him mercilessly for not learning to hunt. A neighbor who suspected that Pete was being abused took him from the owner - who was only more than

110

happy to have him out of his life - and that is how he came to stay with us. I had really gotten attached to Pete and looked forward every day to just loving on him..... As a result of living with his abuser - Pete had developed what I call a Velcro Chin - he would attach it securely to someone who would keep petting him and showing him attention. He was a lover - who found solace and comfort in the arms of any human who did not hurt him. And, after speaking with Mark, and praying a little prayer to God for confirmation - I knew that Pete and Mark had to end up together.

I knew I would really miss Pete - but I also knew that God had a special future in mind for such a special dog. (Deep down - I know I cannot keep all the dogs who come through the rescue - but Pete was one I wouldn't have minded staying for a few more months)....God's timing is always perfect - and somehow I knew Pete's fate was more than likely with Mark.

The following Thursday - Mark arrived at the shop to meet Pete. Mark was early and I retrieved Pete from the back room and let them alone to bond while I let the other dogs outside. When I got back to the front room - Mark was seated on the floor with Pete hanging over his shoulder with that Velcro Chin securely attached around Mark's neck. Mark looked up at me with tears in his eyes.

It was then I noticed his hat. It bore the name of his platoon and some pins on it that reflected his pride in his service days from so very long ago. I remembered him recounting his stories of his post-war platoon and I could not help but think that all of that horror had made this brave man seek his peace and healing in gentleness. I again got a chill of confirmation from God when I was reminded of Pete's past. Pete had endured horrors of his own - and the spark between these two was undeniable. Their shared need for affection and gentleness made for a great fit - the perfect fit.

Mark did not hide his tears in shame - but let them fall on Pete's soft white coat and the two were quiet for a moment - just lost in the soft light shining in the windows of the shop and the need to get familiar with each other's scent. "You wanna come home with me?" Mark whispered to Pete...and the wag of Pete's Tail and his attempts to snuggle closer to Mark was all the answer either of us needed. Pete was going home with Mark - no trouble at all!!!

Every time I place a rescued doggie with a person who comes looking to love it is always a special occasion ....but there are some adoptions and placements that get into my heart. The occasion is even more special - and replays in my mind - releasing my heart to joy and bringing tears to my eyes with its relived memory. Mark and Pete is one of those adoption stories. For it was clearly an occasion that arose out of need, a Divine Appointment for healing, and a placement for peace. I have since heard from Mark twice - both times - he was talking to me with Pete by his side - the Velcro Chin was resting on Mark's chest and I could hear them both breathing in the phone to let me know their symbiotic partnership had made them both complete – healing from horror – by the Divine Plan of Love.

"Who teaches us more than the beasts of the earth and makes us wiser than the birds of the heavens?" Job 35:11

"Double Rescue!!"

Not long ago - I rescued 4 large 5 year-old lab females from a breeder. They all got homes almost immediately - except for Snickers - the overweight white lab who'd had too many puppies in her day - and was now unable to produce babies. Snickers was a great dog - and would walk along beside me without a leash when we went out. She sometimes got a little excited and would jump straight up in the air - looking like a chubby little girl playing jump rope. She was just adorable!!! But people were not appreciative of her zest for life or her size - and despite over 10 showings to people - and about 5 no-shows in Akron - Snickers - unlike her much luckier - and slimmer siblings - remained a rescue without a forever home.

Enter Sandi Yoxtheimer - a friend of Mr. And Mrs. Brad Broad. The Broads brought Sandi over to the new shop the other night because Sandi - a fellow dog rescuer - was wanting to donate some food and supplies to the rescue. I was so very happy to meet her and show them all how the shop was coming along. We were taking a walk through the rescue room - when Sandi stopped in her tracks and looked out the window at the back dog run - where Snickers was sunbathing. She said "What is that?" I laughed and said "Oh - that is poor Snickers - she has been getting her mail here for too long." Sandi went out and started talking with Snickers as Brad's wife turned to me and said "Sandi just lost her white lab, Lucy in February." Then I understood Sandi's instant attraction.

As we followed Sandi outside - we found her crouched down and talking to Snickers - putting her hand through the kennel fence to touch her. I walked up and unlatched the gate saying, "She won't run off. This dog will stay right with you." Snickers instinctively bounded up to Sandi and jumped in the air. Sandi walked around the back yard of the shop with Snickers - remarking how much she looked like Lucy. She even showed me on her phone - pictures of Lucy - and I was amazed that Lucy had about the same body weight as Snickers. She even had the same brown and pink nose. We laughed at how Snickers just kept putting her head into Sandi's hands and sitting in front of her - leaning her back against Sandi's legs and wiggling close to her - as if she couldn't get close enough. Snickers also was much more calm with Sandi than she had been with any other people she had interacted with....almost sensing Sandi's longing for her own Lucy - and trying to comfort her.

Brad and his wife started asking Sandi if she would like to take Snickers home. I had told Brad's wife that I could not imagine Snickers with anyone else - and it was obvious that - though Snickers was a reminder of Lucy - She and Sandi had already formed a bond of their own. Sandi came back to where we were talking inside the shop and I asked her more about Lucy - to see if she might be able and ready to take on Snickers. Sandi spoke of Lucy's passing - how she had just died suddenly while she was out shopping and that she had found her on the kitchen floor - already gone when she came home. The whole time Sandi was telling me this - Snickers was sitting in front of her - listening and looking at her with a dumb grin on her face that let her big tongue hang out her mouth like "ok - now take me home."

"But I had said when she passed....no more! I have other dogs at the house and they each have their own job and their own friends inside the pack...this might disrupt things. I said no more."

It was a standoff - Snickers was staring at Sandi - and Sandi was staring at Snickers. Sandi said "I know you are not Lucy...but what are the odds that I'd find you and you need a home...." More staring ensued.....Finally -

114

Sandi said "Ok - Snickers......Snickers Yoxtheimer! I'll be back to get you tomorrow."

I think Snickers and I both jumped straight in the air. Yay!! A home for Snickers!! And a new baby for Sandi - so much like her lost little girl Lucy - but so new and wonderful in her own ways.

Early afternoon - the very next day - Sandi came to pick up Snickers. She bounded into Sandi's SUV. Sandi and I exchanged hugs and tears and off they went. Later that night - I got an email from Sandi:

"Absolutely, MY GIRL...she is doing fantastic.....in house, she is glued to me. Does not leave my side. Gets along with pug, English Setter and collie mix very well.... She will most likely be sleeping with me too. She is so good in the house I doubt I will worry about crate. LOVE HER with all my heart!!"

I am sure that Snickers loves you, too Sandi. For you both needed each other so much ....and you found each other here. I cannot tell you how happy I am to have been a part of this.....as my rescued dog - and my new rescuer friend have quite obviously rescued one another!!

"Behold, God is my salvation; I will trust, and will not be afraid; for the Lord God is my strength and my song, and he has become my salvation." Isaiah 12:2

"The Selection Process"

I am always amazed at the different ways that people come to pick out a puppy. Sometimes people laugh and they just get caught up in the joy of life as the young and innocent pups run around - jumping and playing. Sometimes, they gravitate towards one in particular and that is it - their mind is made up and they don't even look at another puppy. Some are more methodical - looking for good character traits and good form.....Last night - I had a very strange and new experience with a couple who I met at the new shop to pick out a puppy.

I met Pat and her hubby at the shop at 6 and brought all the puppies out into the back kennel so that they could watch them run around. Both Pat and her husband were very very quiet as they watched them all. They didn't talk - and when they did - they didn't talk very loud. They did not seem to smile much - and they had no real affect.....I was a little worried.

When I was finished bringing out the pups - Pat got into the kennel and her hubby stayed on the outside and passed a few puppies back and forth to each other. Pat had picked up the yellow girl puppy a few times and put her back down. I watched from a distance - so they could be alone and interact with the puppies....but I did notice that every time she put the yellow puppy down - the little girl pup would boldly go back to Pat and climb on her leg....forcing Pat to interact with her. I went inside and said a little prayer to God that one of these puppies would do for them whatever it was they needed to have done. I could not understand why they were not more excited about picking out a puppy....but I just figured that this might have been a manner of selection with which I was not more familiar.

When I returned again - Pat was standing outside the kennel and looking in at the puppies. She had her hand against the kennel - and the yellow pup was pushing all of the other puppies out of the way so that she could be close to Pat's hand. Pat looked up at me very shyly and asked - "Do you have a box or something to take her home?" I laughed and said to Pat...."She kind of chose YOU - didn't she?" and for the first time - Pat smiled.

I got a box and put a blanket inside of it and handed the box to Pat's hubby who carefully placed the puppy in the box and said "Here you go little girl...You are going home."

I hugged Pat and told her that I was so happy that they were chosen by such a special little puppy....and at that - Pat's eyes filled with tears. She told me how they had to put their beagle, Rudy down a year and a half ago - and how they had pretty much cried every day since he had passed. "We never had children - and he was our baby for sixteen years," she said. "But you can't spend a lifetime crying - and he wouldn't want us to be so sad. We are just getting over it and we thought it was time to get another one." I turned to look at Pat's husband and he was wiping his eyes.

And then I finally understood. Selecting a puppy for this particular couple came with much trepidation and sorrow. It was truly the final act of letting go of Rudy, their beloved beagle. It was not something they were completely happy to do because they still missed their baby....but had decided to also let go of some of the past and look ahead to what might be their next baby...their new love. This puppy represented to them the truth that Rudy was really gone - but also gave them hope that they might grow together as a family and share some of what they'd had with Rudy.

I hugged Pat again and she smiled through her tears at the little puppy - wiggling in the box on the front seat - who was just then popping her head up out of the box and looking at Pat as if to say "Let's go!!" Pat laughed and I told her "I hope she is your baby for the next 16 years." Pat's hubby laughed - "Then she will outlive us!" He said.

And they climbed in the car - Pat driving, and her husband holding the little girl in the blanket as they drove away - both kissing her and smiling at her and talking to her. I am sure somewhere over the rainbow bridge - Rudy was smiling down on them, too. One of his little cousins had just gotten a home with the only wonderful people he had ever known....and knowing what good parents they were - I'm sure he wouldn't have it any other way.

"May the God of hope fill you with all joy and peace in believing, so that by the power of the Holy Spirit you may abound in hope." Romans 15:13

"The Chuggle"

I got so many messages about Sadie - the cute little Chuggle...I was overwhelmed with the response just as - it seemed – everyone was apparently overwhelmed with Sadie's cuteness. But no one was perhaps as overwhelmed as a woman named Cathy. Cathy and her husband - who are raising their granddaughter, Tiara - have been looking for a small dog for her for a little while. Early yesterday morning - Cathy's messages started coming through. And then her text messages. They really wanted this dog and they wanted to see her as soon as possible. I thought - this woman is relentless...but I had not yet heard Cathy's reasons...I had not yet heard Tiara's story.

Cathy told me that Tiara wanted to be in 4-H next year and they had been looking for a little dog that she could train. She said they also wanted to get her a dog because Tiara was going to be facing surgery soon - and they wanted her to have a cuddle buddy when she returned from the hospital. First of all, I thought that maybe Tiara was much older - Cathy never told me how old she was - but I assumed pre-teen. She also told me that the surgery was to correct a genetic defect in her legs that allowed her hips to swivel 90 degrees and that she needed the surgery so her joints would not suffer damage as she grew and got older. So I am thinking the whole time - 12 year old - wants to be in 4-H - cuddle buddy - cute little dog. No problem. So we agreed to meet in the evening for them to meet Sadie.

And who shows up but this tiny firecracker of a girl with the most infectious personality ever....Tiara - beautiful and bubbly and so loving and energetic. I looked at Cathy and said "How old is she?" "I'm 8!" Tiara piped right up and told me. I couldn't believe it. "And this is the little girl

119

with the leg problem?" I asked....watching her run all over the shop - waiting to meet Sadie? I went and got her - and watched Tiara chase her until Sadie settled down and landed right in Tiara's lap.

"Yes" Cathy answered - and Tiara got up and showed me how her legs could rotate a full 90 degrees from front to back because of the joints in her hip. "Doesn't it hurt?" I asked. And Cathy told me - not until recently - that is how they knew she needed surgery. And then I asked "So what will they do?" Cathy then looked up at me from the chair where they were snuggling Sadie and told me "Well - they have been trying to do the least invasive thing - but now are sure they are going to have to be broken and reset so they will heal correctly." This news made me wince. Oh to think of that beautiful and energetic little girl having to have both of her hips broken and reset. To spend that much time recovering...and to be still for that long.

I watched Tiara with Sadie - who was already attached to her lap. She snuggled her and said to Cathy "Can we go? I want to take my puppy home and call all my friends." Tears filled my eyes as I thought about her surgery. I was comforted to know that Sadie the chug would be there to cuddle Tiara and help her through the rough days ahead. And I quickly tried to pull myself together. Because I could not imagine that Tiara would understand why anyone would cry over her situation. To her it was all pretty simple. "I am having surgery, and cuddling with my doggie, and then I am going to train her and show her in 4-H" She said.

So it was done deal....she was getting her puppy and Sadie was getting a forever home. Two happy and bubbly souls were being united - and despite the uncertainties of their pasts - their futures looked amazingly bright and held so much hope together. Sadie and Tiara were already bonded - kissing and hugging on the shop room floor.

"Did you tell Rita what you are going to train the dog for?" Cathy asked Tiara

Tiara smiled that amazing smile up at me and said "I want her to be a therapy dog to go to the hospitals and visit with people, so that they will be happy."

More tears filled my eyes - and I felt that "God-tug" on my heart that happens when I know that everything is going to be alright. I knew if anyone could make those people happy - it would be Tiara - and that Sadie would just be icing on the cake. But then again - what is cake without icing? I had a feeling that together - Tiara and Sadie would make lots of people happy!!

"I have said these things to you, that in me you may have peace. In the world you will have tribulation. But take heart; I have overcome the world." John 16:13

"That One Dog..."

Yesterday, an old fella named Ed drove about 45 miles to come down to the rescue to see "Spring" - our Schipperke mix who literally jumps like she has "springs" on her feet! He had called me earlier in the day and had told me at length about his little dog "Chops" who had passed away a year and a half ago....Chops was a Schipperke and Pug mix - a very unique looking dog, indeed....The more I listened - I also realized that Chops was unique in other ways....Despite cancer and a whole list of other ailments - Chops had lived to be 14...He rode in a side-car in Ed's motorcycle, and wore goggles and scarf....and he knew a bunch of tricks that Ed had taught him that he could perform with ease until the day he died.

"That's how we knew something was wrong with him. He just kept walking in circles," Ed said tearfully - "By the time we got him to the vet - it was too late and he passed from something in his brain...."Ed told me that he had been looking for a schipperke mix for the past year - and he couldn't find one who came even close to Chops. I invited him down to look at Spring - even though I told him she had no pug in her - but was a nice and fiesty little dog nonetheless...."Well - So was Chops" he said - "I'll come down."

When Ed arrived at the rescue, I knew who he was immediately - A Big old fella wearing overalls and boots - he had thick red cheeks and hardly any hair. He reminded me of Edgar Winters - and I said to him "You're Ed!" He smiled. I was just finishing up with some people who'd adopted a puppy - and Ed waited for me by petting and talking to the other dog "greeters" at the shop.

After the puppy adopters went happily on their way - I got to talk with Ed. He showed me pictures of his little Chops - and told me what a great dog he was - and how he had been looking for a dog like him pretty much ever since he died...."Well - I'll go get Spring" I said.

The moment Spring came through the door - I knew it was not going to be a match....Ed's face fell and he shook his head "Nope, That is not what I am looking for." He said.....I smiled and I patted his arm. "I didn't think so...." I replied - watching his hope dissolve into disappointment. "I mean....she's a really cute dog...." He said....'But she's not Chops....' I wanted so badly to say to him....

I also wanted to say "No dog is going to be Chops....because your time with Chops has passed away with him...." I wanted to say "I am so so sorry that you lost your beloved little dog...and that dog was so lucky to be loved by such a sweet wonderful man who misses him so much....." I wanted to say " I am so sorry that I cannot squat right down and make from the dust and dog hair on the floor a new Chops that will take his place and be just like the old Chops....But I can't" I want so badly to be able to do that for him. But I couldn't.....

All I could do was stand there and watch his sweet face fall and his hopes be dashed by the knowledge that this dog was not going to take his dog's place. He squared his shoulders against his disappointment and handed me ten dollars...."

Here's a donation for your time" he said. "And God bless you people who rescue dogs"

I thanked him and watched his big frame pass through the door and get into his truck.

I knew exactly how he felt.....I think we all do....

Because we all have a Chops in our Dog-Loving history....A dog who makes us laugh, a dog who we believe God created just for us...a dog who wormed their way deep into our soul and who will be with us until the day we join them at the rainbow bridge....

For me that is Hannah, for my kids, that dog is Lucy, and I could sit here and write list after list of people who loved a dog like Chops and have tried countless times to "Replace" that brand of kinship with an animal....Sometimes we can - and sometimes we can't.....

Believe me - if I could change the life span of dogs and have them live longer than we live - I certainly would do just that....But I can't....And I am not about to take that one up with God....He knows way better than I do why dogs lives are so short and ours are so long....

But maybe He intended it that way because He knew that there were going to be so many dogs who needed homes...who needed us to love them - and to not be afraid to take a chance on that kind of love again....I looked down at Spring who looked up at me with great concern....I said to her "Don't worry - you didn't do anything wrong....." And I hugged her and kissed her and took her back to the rescue room....Praying the whole way that someday -someone would love her - not only for the rest of her life - but also for the rest of theirs.....

"So also you have sorrow now, but I will see you again, and your hearts will rejoice, and no one will take your joy from you." John 16:22

"A Lovey Old Hound"

"We came to see the hound..." Frank said....He and his wife Deborah had come all the way from Akron on her day off and had just shown up at the rescue without an appointment and without us having any knowledge that they were coming.

"Hound?" I asked

"Yes - Lillie!" Frank said. "We saw her on the website and she is just beautiful!"

Lillie!! My mind raced - No one ever comes to see Lillie....No one ever wants to adopt a hound dog! I looked around for Lillie - remembering that I had just put her outside...

"She is a Treeing Walker Coonhound...." I said, gathering up a leash to go out and get her...

Frank looked confused ...."Yes - I know!" He replied....

My eyes narrowed and I poked him in the arm "You plan on hunting her?....Because she doesn't hunt!" I said poking him with each final syllable to make my point....

Lillie had come to us off the street....State Rt. 21 to be exact. Some wonderful lady found her running up and down the highway - frantically looking for her people who had undoubtedly left her in the middle of the road where she had been dumped. The wonderful lady had brought her to us and had asked that we either find her original owners - if by some chance they had NOT dumped her and would ever come looking for her...or find her a good home someday....And so six months later - she was still with us....

She had been just skin and bones back then - and had become even more thin and gaunt after a bout with an upper respiratory infection nearly killed her in early August....Still - Lillie pulled out of her illnesses and had turned into a beautiful and loving dog. She had filled out, calmed down, and had become a regal looking creature who was just the love of the rescue....

The volunteers, the frequent visitors, and everyone who knew her at Here Doggie Doggie had become her immediate family. We were ever so protective of her - and did not want to see her go to a hunter - since we were not sure if she had ever hunted - and especially now since she had become such a "house dog".

"NO! I am not going to hunt her...." Frank protested my fervent screening of his intentions for Lillie...."I am retired and want to just hang out with her....The wife still works but I am home all day and night....I love Walkers - always had one in the house when I was little and even hunted some with them...." Frank went on "But there is nothing better than a lovey old hound!"

"We came down on my day off..." Deborah added "We both want her..." she said..

I smiled at him and said "Well, Okay then...."

And I went out and gathered up Lillie on a lead for her to meet Frank and Deborah....

Once inside again...Lillie approached the couple cautiously....She sized them up and looked up at them inquisitively with her regal face and sniffed Franks hand when he offered it to her....

"She is just beautiful!" Frank whispered....and then he sat down on a nearby chair and offered his lap to her by tapping the tops of his legs with his hands....

"Lillie.." He said softly - and slowly - Lillie crawled up to his lap and laid her whole body across him as he stroked her ears and her face as if he had just re-discovered a family heirloom or had unearthed a long-forgotten treasure...

"Nope," Frank said shaking his head and looking at her as if he was holding a true work of art...."There is just nothing like a lovey old hound. She is just a gorgeous girl!"

Lillie began to relax and bond with Frank....She pawed at his arms and laid across his lap as if she felt she belonged there.....Then Frank bestowed upon her the ultimate gift of ownership - a brand new collar and a leash that he and Deborah had purchased just for her - before they ever even saw her....
"We fell in love with her picture - but it didn't do her justice." Frank said

And then Frank said those magical words that all dogs in rescue wait to hear:
"Do you want to come home with me?" he said - stroking her face and looking into her amazingly gentle brown eyes....At this - Lillie stood up and lead Frank toward the door....
The volunteers who were there that day stood there moist eyed and so very happy for Lillie - Knowing that in many ways her journey in rescue has just come to a close - but in so many other ways - her new and exciting life had just begun...
Lillie literally clung to Frank's side and excitedly looked up at Deborah as they made their way to the door...."Nope - "said Frank "No doubt about it at all....This one was supposed to be my girl! Let's go home Lillie"
Before that day - no one ever came asking to see Lillie....Not many people ever want to adopt a Hound Dog....But as "Hound lovers" - Frank and Deborah knew and appreciated what an amazingly beautiful hound our Lillie truly was....and they knew exactly how lucky they were - as "Hound people" to be taking her home.

"We love because he first loved us." 1John 4:19

"Rescued Dog "

We really didn't know much what to think about Sadie when she came to us....She as an older Lab and Shepherd mix...Fast on her feet and slow to warm up to us. She came in with four pregnant females who were hungry - for both food and affection - and had been dumped in the country along Mottice Drive outside of Waynesburg. The poor fella whose property had been their dumping ground brought them in to us in September - just as the nights began to get cold. "I think they are all bred..." He'd said to us - "They were dumped several weeks ago - but my grandkids named them all" And Sadie was the name they had given this pretty girl who came to us - pregnant and unwanted...so the name stuck.

She was a nipper at first. We were worried about other dogs and even sometimes ourselves because she was not happy in her situation - and who could blame her! Pregnant - dumped - put in and out of a crate in rescue...being let out with other dogs who wanted to play and get to know her - when all she wanted to do was sulk in her depression and cry. Often she took out her sadness on other dogs or on us by nipping and growling. We knew in time she would trust us - but until she did - we had to be very careful of her attitudes and her swing temperament. We were careful about her - but gave her just as much love as she could handle given her delicate situation.

A few days after Thanksgiving, Sadie gave birth to two puppies - fat and rollie-pollie. One was brown and fuzzy like a teddy bear - and one was all white - just like her. One boy and one girl. As a mom - Sadie flourished....I think it was the first time that she felt safe because she allowed us to clean her pups and her cage while she watched us carefully. She also got to dart outside for a little break from the motherhood vigil of nursing and childcare - and every time she came back in - her pups were fine and we were standing by as good babysitters. Sadie began rewarding us with her love and kisses....and even after her little ones grew up and got homes - her trust for us grew. She became a dog we could love on and she gave us love back.

One of the happiest improvements we could see in Sadie was that she began to play. It is always a happy day when a frightened and depressed dog finally picks up a toy and chases it or throws it up in the air with joy - because we know that she is just being a dog. She is done with being frightened and afraid and not knowing if she will be hurt or misused...and she can just relax and do what a dog is supposed to do....Play....like a child...when innocence returns and she knows she is loved and cared for. Sadie played - and we loved the slight smile that had started to grow on her face and the soft expression that played now on her brow. Sadie was at last ready to be trusted as the good dog she was and was ready to find a good home.

That home came this week when one of our volunteers, Marie, brought in a sweet lady who had been looking for a good dog to bring in her home...This wonderful woman has a condition that makes it difficult for her to walk very fast, and her husband wanted her to have a dog that could protect her and also fit in with the other little dog in the home. Marie directed her to our Facebook page, and she and her husband both took an instant liking to Sadie.

"We had a yellow lab before, and Sadie has that kind and sweet face. She is older, too which really makes us happy because we wanted to rescue but did not want a puppy."
Marie set up a meeting and this week the lady and Sadie met.

It was amazing - because Sadie seemed to instinctively know that her new owner might not be able to move very fast...and though Sadie was quite the runner and could move through the rescue like lightning...she sidled up to our new friend peacefully and slowly.

The lady sat in a chair for a good part of the meeting - and she never left the lady's side. She parked her body in front of her and stood between her and us - as if her duties of protection had already begun. The lady loved her immediately and we knew it was a match that only God could have dreamed up in His divine and heavenly fashion for both of them.

The next day - Sadie's new mom brought her dad along to seal the deal. Sadie was as crazy about him as she was her new mom. As I bathed Sadie for the last time and got her ready for her trip to her new home - she shook with excitement. No doubt she knew she had been chosen for adoption...and she was going to her new home.

What a huge difference from the first moments Sadie arrived in the doors of the rescue to the last moments when she pressed her nose against the glass to make her exit....What a happy and excited dog now stood in the place where a shamed and unwanted dog had once been. Sadie was no longer unwanted. She had indeed been transformed and made ready for a job that God no doubt had intended for her special qualities all along....And she walked out the door...ready to love, trust, protect, and even play....Not just a rescue dog...but a Rescued Dog - in every way.

"For if while we were enemies we were reconciled to God by the death of his Son, much more, now that we are reconciled, shall we be saved by his life." Romans 5:10

"Joyful Abandon!"

Angie showed up at the rescue today - to bring us the remaining food and medicine from her dog who had just passed away a few weeks ago. We both got very teary eyed as she told me about her beloved old dog Jerry. How much he had suffered with his bad hip dysplasia...how he'd fallen asleep in her arms as the vet administered the sedative just before he was euthanized. She told me about how his ashes had just arrived and how the pain from losing him was still so raw...and that she was thinking...not sure if she was ready yet.....but still thinking about getting a dog from us to help ease her pain when she was ready.

She told me all of this while Socks - the dog who had just been dropped off by her owner played at her feet and insisted on being by her side. Just an hour before - Socks had lost someone important to her as well. Her owner - who had adopted her from us almost 9 months ago - dropped her off at the door - saying that his work schedule had gotten to be too involved and that he could no longer keep her. For that hour in the rescue - Socks wondered around jumping up on us and demanding our attention as if to say "What is going on here? What did I do? Where did he go?" We felt so bad for her and we were so angry at the way that she was abandoned, that Angie's story of losing her own beloved dog made us even sadder. Here was one doggie - literally thrown away...and yet another doggie- whose owner stood before us with tears in her eyes telling us that she would have given anything if she could have kept him alive - just a bit longer.

And as Angie spoke to us about Jerry - she kept petting Socks ...and telling her that she was such a pretty girl and that she felt so bad for her...Socks gave Angie Kisses - as if to say "I'm so sorry that you lost your best friend.....I know exactly how you feel...." And as I watched the two of them - I seriously hoped that maybe a bond would be formed....that maybe Angie would feel that she was ready...and that maybe their two hearts could be healed in the company of one another..

Angie promised that she would come back next week and bring her daughter. She said she would think about Socks and have her daughter look at her on line. She stayed till almost closing time today - talking about Jerry...And as Angie walked out the door I told her that Jerry still was around and would be happy if she could get over his passing over the rainbow bridge....I told her that He probably already knew that his friends who were still alive and needed homes on this earth would love to have a great doggie mom such as her to love them and care for them. I told her to stay positive and that life is good....

And about 10 minutes later - just as we were locking the doors - Angie called me - frantically asking if we were still there.

"Yes...."I replied "Did you forget something?" I asked her.

She spoke quickly and excitedly "I am coming back for Socks!" She said.

And I was so happy....

For in a very few moments - Socks was seated in the lap of her new best friend. Socks and Angie held each other and sat in front of the shop - kissing each other and looking at each other as if it were too good to be true....Because what was once a sad day for both of them - had turned to joy....They had both been somewhat lost...And now by the miracle of God's timing had found each other...Forever Healed and Forever Home.

"Rejoice in the Lord always; again I will say, Rejoice. " Philippians 4:4

"A Chief's Desire"

He served our country - in the Navy - for twenty plus years. He saw all kinds of death and devastation which hardened his heart, gave him a rough and demanding demeanor, and made him appear to be, well, somewhat of a dick - for lack of a better word. But Chief Petty Officer Donald - who regularly skimmed our shop for a little girl Pug Dog - really only longed for love...The four legged, warm fuzzy fur kind of love that he had once known - and now was trying desperately to find again. And he placed this difficult task in the hands of Here Doggie Doggie.

After retiring from the Navy - several years back, Chief - as everyone calls him - had been blessed enough to be chosen by a little black pug mix who came wandering up to his truck - abandoned and alone one day in the middle of a shopping center parking lot. Chief opened up his door and called to her - and she jumped into his truck - and stayed in his life for over 13 years. Sadly, though, because dogs who should really live forever always die way before their masters, Chief lost his little "Dorrie Ann" about a year ago - and it "damn near killed him" in his own words....He couldn't talk about her without his eyes getting all misty - even though he still growled like a junk yard dog when he spoke to us.

Often Chief would come looking for another pug or pug mix - something that would give him the same kind of feeling that he had found with Dorrie Ann....and every time he pulled in front of our shop - we would cringe a little....because Chief was ...well....Chief. He related to us the way he would his underlings in the Navy. He would call us out on why we hadn't contacted him about this dog or that dog that looked "Pug-like" ...but then after spending time with each dog that he thought he'd like - he would say "Nope...when I see her - I'll know." He really put us through our paces!!

Then one day a beautiful little pug came to us from a pug breeder lady who had moved and had five dogs in her care...Some were her kids dogs...some were hers...but she needed to "thin the herd" - as she put it (which kills us) - but whatever! When I entered the shop with the little pug dog under my arm – our volunteer named "Fuzz" looked at me and said "No way! There was just a guy here - he said you call 'crazy Navy guy' ...crabbin and bitchin - said he wanted a pug." I started to laugh and said - "Oh yeah - I know who it is." Fuzz said - "You gonna call him?" and I told her I would. But I never got a chance to make the phone call...because the next place I stopped that day I ran right into him. "Hey Chief Don," I said walking up to him....

"Crazy Red Head!!" He replied "I was just at your place."

I laughed and told him I was out picking up the prettiest little pug I had ever seen and his face changed...

"Really?" He asked....Misty expression noted...

I said "Yes sir, and you'd better get into see her right away because this one won't be there long...she is gorgeous! We open at 9 in the morning"

"Nine? Hell I'm not even up at Nine!!!" He growled.

I just gave him a hug and smiled and told him "I'll see you tomorrow."

Sure enough at a little after nine, Chief arrived with his sister in tow and a huge bag of dog food for the shelter. He stood still as I released the little pug girl from her cage and she came running out and jumping all over him. I knew it had to be a match made in heaven...but even so - Chief had to look her over really good and grumble a little about how she was nothing like Dorrie Ann...

I looked at him and I said "Look, you are not going to find another Dorrie Ann. This dog will give you new adventures - just like Dorrie Ann...Take her home - try her out - and if you like her - come sign the paper work....and if you don't - bring her back. That's the best I can do...and she loves you. Just look at her!!!"

We looked down and she was wagging her tail like crazy - looking up at him with her big huge Puggie eyes. Chief Don reached down and picked her up and said "Ok Sis - Let's give this girl a try..." He said he would be back in a few days to let me know.Well, Chief Don may have appeared to be a rough and gruff dick of a fellow - for lack of a better word - but once he had his new doggie in his care...I believe that his heart became somewhat mushy. The same day that Chief Donald took the dog home - I received several anxious phone calls worried about what kind of food she'd been eating because he couldn't get her to eat...So I called her old owner and asked and called him back and told him...

"Hell - I've bought four different foods...I thought she was going to starve!!" he said. I laughed shaking my head...Chief sounded completely different with this new pug in his care.

In a few days - Chief and his sister came back in the shop. The Pug had a new collar and a sweet little pink leash and a new name. "I call her Baby Girl" Chief said with a little smile on his lips. He carefully put her on the ground and walked her outside of the shop to go potty...and he said "She has a vet's appointment in an hour - right up the street. No more puppies for her," he said.

We stood outside and talked for a bit - he did most of the talking - to baby girl...but I observed a distinct change in Chief. He spoke sweetly and he seemed really at peace with this little girl in his arms. I couldn't help but think it was a divine appointment - running into him the same day that the little girl Pug came into our rescue. Of course I never even pretend to know what God has planned for our little doggies and their future families - but I always know that it will be a happy beginning for both of them.

"But rejoice insofar as you share Christ's sufferings, that you may also rejoice and be glad when his glory is revealed. "   1 Peter 4:13

"Sister-Sister"

They were sisters....part Pomeranian and part Maltese.....The two Pom-Tese were bonded by being born into the same litter and their bond cemented by being adopted and brought up by the same wonderful lady. The lady kept them ten years....and she treated them like royalty....She had them spade - they were housebroken and they were given lots of treats.....In the evenings - the sisters loved to sit with the lady and love on her when they were all alone after the lady's grandchildren and children's visits for the day were over. Life with the lady was nice and comfortable....and warm and loving....Then - last year - the lady died....

The Lady had a friend who promised to take the Pom-Tese sisters if ever anything happened ...and so the friend got them when the lady died.....and she had them for just a few weeks before she started having her own health issues and had to, herself - move into a nursing facility. This left the two Pom-Tese sisters homeless....and - like so many other homeless doggies in the valley - the Pom-Tese sisters came to Here Doggie Doggie - in search of a new home.

The first month or so - the " Pom Girls" as we called them - were terribly depressed....not only had their own human mommy passed away - but their foster mommy - who they knew well - had gone away abruptly and without explanation....At the rescue they were aloof from us. They stared at us wide-eyed and would not come near us.....but over time - a very long time - they started to trust us....We would bring them treats and they started to respond by putting their little feet up on us when we would let them out to potty and for playtime and meals. They never really let us pick them up - but they eventually showed us that they longed for human touch....they longed to be loved...and they actually missed the connection shared by living with people by jumping up on us and allowing us to love them back....

They became like family to us - because - time passed - and still more passed...and we began to get afraid for them...I mean - these girls were 10 years old....in great shape - absolutely!....but even in the realm of "cute and fuzzy" -

older dogs never get picked first. ...especially when circumstance makes it impossible for them to be split up. ...We started to think they might become just permanent pets at the rescue - which is truly no life for an older dog - especially those used to being spoiled!! But all of that changed this past weekend - when I received a text from our volunteer named Fuzz Kuhens...She told me about a lady she had been talking to about adopting a little dog....She said this lady's name was Florence and she had adopted one of our old-aged dogs a year ago and who had, sadly, lost him this year to heart problems..... Florence was looking for another dog - and when told about the "Pom Girls" - she decided to meet them....BOTH!!!

Today the "Pom-Girls" had their meet and greet with Florence....and when I walked into the rescue a few hours after Florence had met them - Fuzz met us at the door telling us "The Pom Girls are gone...Florence took them with her!" I was overwhelmed with a sense of peace and thankfulness....The Pom girls had a new home...and not just any home - A home where their new lady was a dog lover....a lady who already loved older dogs and knew all about spoiling and loving homeless doggies who may be scared or sick, or challenged in some way by their advanced age.....The right lady that would come along at the right time...and love these girls for who they are.
Tonight I got a text message from Fuzz that included a picture of the "Pom Girls" - sitting with a wonderful lady whose home is nice and comfortable ...and warm and loving....and who they - apparently - will sit and love on in the evenings when visits from the lady's grandchildren and children are over and ....they can feel safe and happy and very much welcome....Where they will not have to be separated for any reason - until their passing over the rainbow bridge....Because this wonderful lady wanted them both - and will keep their bond as sisters sacred - for the rest of their lives.

"Say to wisdom, "You are my sister," and call insight your intimate friend," Proverbs 7:4

"Buffalo Girl"

Emory showed up with a dozen or so other children from the elementary school to visit the doggies and start some special projects in which the group is participating in the next school year. Along with the group, Emory sat in the front room of the rescue and received instructions from the group leaders, and - like most of the other children present that day - his attention wandered from what the leaders were saying to the stacks of cages containing various pooches that they were going to walk as part of their group project. Unlike the others, however, Emory became fixated on one particular dog - a shy sweet yorkie poo who we had started calling "Buffalo Girl" - because the huge tangles and mats in her fur made the front of her body appear big and burly like a buffalo. "Buffalo Girl" - or "Buffy" for short - was a rescued mom from a puppy mill where she had given birth to lots of pups for profit - but had never had a real home of her own. As a result of not having much attention in her life, she was shy but longed for human touch - and for some reason - she spotted Emory and became as enchanted with him as he was with her.

After the groups initial instructions, Emory asked if he could take Buffy out of her cage and play with her. We of course agreed, knowing that Buffy was both harmless and starved for attention and thought her time with Emory would be good for her. Throughout the hour and a half that the group was there, Emory played only with Buffy...He held her and loved on her the whole time. When they played - she danced around him and - though she ran around the front room of the rescue with the other children - Buffy always came back to Emory and would jump up on his legs - asking for more of his gentle hugs and kisses. When the school group left, I remember Emory telling one of the volunteers that he longed for a dog like her....and he said of all of the dogs there that day - he loved her the most.

Fast Forward a month...the children had come and gone and many other people had come looking for dogs at the rescue. Buffy had been taken out and played with probably a dozen times and put back because she was either "Too

Big"...."Too Old" "Too Fat" to be adopted by other people's standards. Buffy had seen all of her Puppy Mill mates adopted before her. We couldn't quite figure it out - because she had been shaved down, bathed, and prettied up since she first came in all "Buffalo-like".....but still no one had yet adopted her. It was just one of those 'inexplicables' where we all just figure she would go when God found the right person for her. Unless - of course the right person had already found her!

Tuesday I received a call from my bestie Christine as driving back to the rescue after an appointment in the afternoon. "Someone is here to adopt Buffy and I just wanted to ask you a few things...." She told me that it was a boy who had been here with the school group a month ago and his mom. "The mom says he has not stopped talking about her - and she told him if she was still here today they would adopt her."

I answered her questions and said what a great thing it was for Buffy to get a home.

"Oh - it sure was!" Christine said "You should have seen her....she danced all around him and jumped up on him - It was like she remembered him...I swear!" I could hear the joy in Christine's voice and I could remember the boy playing with her that day and knew that was probably the reason that Buffy had not gotten adopted before. God was waiting on Emory and Emory's Mom to come and get her.

"What an Awesome thing for that mom to do!" Christine said - and I couldn't agree more!

Last night I received an email from Emory's Mom, Karah...She wanted to update me on Buffy's progress since they took her home. "Our other dogs welcomed her into the "pack" like she has always been here. The kids have been holding her and loving on her. She is in heaven!! She even likes our cats! She is a little nervous and it will definitely take her some time to adjust but she is home! "

She also told me that they decided to call her "May"....which I think is just about the most perfect name for her....because they gave her the only home she ever had and a loving place to live and be loved - all in God's timing - on a day in "May"

Way to go Emory - for falling in love with our Buffalo Girl and refusing to leave her behind....You and your mom have given her the best gift ever - a forever home and all the love she needs to grow into the good baby dog God always knew she could be. And Way to go Buffalo Girl - Now "MAY" - the rest of your life be filled with warm blankets and hugs and kisses and treats. "MAY" you live forever with that darling little boy whose love rescued you .....God Bless you - you are home!

"But to all who did receive him, who believed in his name, he gave the right to become children of God," John 1:12

"Long Awaited Friend"

"I have found myself in a position now where I am all alone...and I can have a dog" Latisha said to me over the phone last Saturday. She was just so tickled because she was going to spend her day "dog shopping" she said. "My daughter lived with me with my grandbaby for three years and she didn't want a dog in the house because of the baby. ...and before that I had a man who hated dogs....guess that should have been a sign..." She sighed....and then her voice picked up "But now I live alone and my daughter got her own place....And I want to get a dog!" I laughed with her because I knew too well about wanting a dog and not being able to have one because of angry men and little babies. I was so glad she called me because I was really hoping to open that door to loving a furbaby again for her.

"Well come on down and shop!" I said to her. I told her our location and she said she would see me sometime in the afternoon.

I knew her very well when she came in - big smile - looking all around at the dogs in the front room who stood barking at her. She could tell they all were hopeful of being held and loved. Almost immediately she gravitated towards one of the Amish rescue yorkie poos who was shy but friendly and very sweet. "I like one of them." Latisha said...and after holding a few other doggies in the shop - she went back to the yorkie poo who had already seemed to "pick" her for its new momma - and she held it very close and looked out under her long lashes and said "Well....I think she's the one!"

We celebrated for a minute - but I had promised to groom the little girl up pretty before she took it home - so I rushed off to the bathing room and scrubbed the little girl clean and soft so I could get her ready for her excited new momma. Now, normally - when I groom up a doggie - the owner stays some distance away and lets me do my thing....but not Latisha. She was there - hands on - showing me what she wanted done and just how short she wanted the hair...She told me how to make her face look and what to do with her feet. I was starting to think that she was being kind of a pain in the butt when I looked over and noticed she was crying.I stopped and put down my grooming shears and comb - completely baffled as to her tears and just hugged her.

She said "I'm sorry...." and sniffed and wiped her eyes "I am just so happy to get this little baby....I am so happy. I have wanted a little dog to love and pamper forever. And this little girl is gonna be so loved...."
Tears also filled my eyes as I realized that what I do day in and day out actually does mean something to other people....and apparently to this beautiful soul - it meant so much. I guess sometimes in doing what is commonplace in our business of placing doggies - I forget that. Because sometimes it is routine - but to each person who comes to us for a dog - we are filling a whole in a heart....We are placing something precious in their hands - and even - quite possibly - fulfilling a dream. I think I was just so busy that day that I forgot that with Latisha - and her tears and her excitement - she reminded me of why God had given me such an opportunity in the first place.

For after the hair was groomed and the feet were trimmed - and after the papers were signed and the fees were exchanged....Latisha held that little yorkie-poo fur-baby and smiled a smile from her soul....Her dream of having a dog had been fulfilled...and her excitement had reignited my appreciation for why I do this rescue thing. For sometimes - we do not always know what the rehoming of a rescue dog means to the new owner - only what it will mean to the dog...Last Saturday - Latisha showed me through her excitement and tears just what it meant to her.

"Don't worry - this little girl will have a great life and will be so spoiled!" She said to me as she kissed her new baby and walked out the door.....
And I replied to her exactly what my heart felt for both of them over what God must have been planning for this very special adoption...."No worries!"

"Delight yourself in the Lord, and he will give you the desires of your heart." Psalm 37:4

"Sweet Caroline!"

So Caroline became a true fixture around the Rescue ....She was a mild mannered sweet dog who listened well and always went outside to go to do her business. Unfortunately - she and another female got into a scrape outside and for a very long time, Caroline retired to the rescue room and refused to go outside. Then her potty habits changed and she became known as our "predictable pooper"....She would come out of her kennel - walk a few laps around the room - pee a big puddle on the floor - and make three piles in a circle....every - single - day. Her predictable antics became laughable to us - and we knew that if she didn't want to go into her kennel to drink her water or eat her food - she probably had one more pile to make before she was ready. She was so sweet that she endeared herself to us as one of our rescue family - even though we had to clean up after her until her fear of going outside finally eased up for her. We just loved her and did what we had to - to make her feel at home.
It is very difficult in rescue for older dogs....They get to watch the little ones come and go. They get to see more desirable and younger dogs move in and out of the shelter quickly. Old dogs take longer because everyone wants a pup to play with...and for the old ones, the rescue does become their home - for a very long time. Caroline watched the coming of fall, and Christmas time, and then the frozen dark days of winter....and while it was good for her to not be out in the elements as she had once been - we all knew that she - like other dogs at the rescue - longed for a real home. People don't usually come looking for an old dog ....They just don't!

In fact, last Saturday - when Josh and his girlfriend and her little girl came walking into the yard at the rescue and looking for a mild mannered dog for his great grandmother and his grandmother's farm - we did not even think about showing them Caroline. We thought about the obvious farm dogs we have....Kanga - who is middle aged but needs some land to run....and Molly - the wonderful Lab mix who is mild mannered but still playful....."These dogs are great..." said Josh..."But my grandmother is 74 and her mother is 96....they had this awesome dog who just was by their side all the time...and she just stayed on the porch and in the front room with them....wherever they were. It passed away and they want another seasoned older dog"....he said.

Finally it dawned on us....."Caroline! Caroline is perfect!!"

So we went to the back room and came back with Caroline - grungy from being outdoors and rolling on the ground. She approached them and sniffed at them.....her tail wagged and she walked right up to the little girl and stood in front of her. I don't know if it was something about their scent or just the fact that they were there to see her - but she immediately attached herself to them and stayed right by them.

The couple asked if they could take her for a walk and she walked perfectly with them - paying close attention to the little girl and being extremely gentle - as was her nature. "She knows!" Josh's girlfriend said...."She really knows...Look at how she is with us."

Caroline's tail wagged and she lifted her head - looking more beautiful than she ever had since being at the rescue.

"I think it's a 'yes'!" Josh said with a smile..."I know my grandmothers - and they are going to love her.

Before I would let them take her - I begged them to let me bathe her. "She is so dirty..." I told them - "I can't let her go like this..." But they insisted that they wanted to take her and give her a bath themselves...."We'll take her to the self-serve bathing place in Philly..." they told me..."We just want to get her to the farm as soon as possible."

So we attached a leash to the new collar we gave her and prepared to say goodbye to her.

There is a strange thing that happens to a rescue dog once a new collar is put on them and their new leash is placed in the hands of the adopter....The dog knows that his or her life is about to change. Caroline was no exception - for as she accepted our loving kisses of goodbye with affection - she turned her nose toward the front door - the only door she had not been let out of ever - and waited with a wagging tail to begin her new life - wherever it was going to take her. We watched as she walked out with her head held very high and walked proudly with the couple and the little girl to their truck and piled in with them and drove off down the road to get the life that she so deserved to have.

At the rescue - of course - we dried our eyes and shared our memories of Caroline's first days with us and how she had come to be "Caroline" with new volunteers who did not even remember when she had not lived in the rescue room. We took to texting our families and the other volunteers on our phones and sharing the miracle of Caroline's adoption. And indeed it was a miracle...for Caroline was an old lady dog - not something that everyone would want like a little yorkie or bichon...she was an undesirable...a tough case...but a love nonetheless...Her story gave all of us at the rescue new hope to find homes for the other Carolines who linger here - and for other dogs who are difficult to place....for we had further confirmation that in God's time and by placing every situation in His hands - there is hope.

That night I received a text from the couple who had come to take Caroline to her new home. it was a picture of Josh's 96 year old great grandmother and his 74 year old grandmother - loving on Caroline - and her receiving their love with a big smile and a huge new bone at her feet. I smiled because I knew that there was no accident in her story - in her being our old rescue dog for so long...because right now - with these two older ladies loving on her and spoiling her - she was again - right where she needed to be.

"And you will know the truth, and the truth will set you free." John 8:32

"Where Blessings Begin"

"So, I think I am in love with the Tri-Pod...." Emily said to me in an instant message over Facebook....She was speaking about Vader - a Black Lab that had come in as an owner-surrender. Vader only had three legs because he had been hit by a car at the tender age of four months....He and his brother Zeus had found themselves at our rescue because their family had recently experienced some health crises that made it difficult to take good care of them - and Zeus had already gotten a really good home. He and Vader were not bonded and did not get along that well....So Vader was still at the rescue - a three-legged homeless dog - who was both beautiful and smart and waiting for someone with a good heart to notice him.

Emily - of course - would be that person.....I had known Emily since the fall - when she began coming with her family to donate and visit with the doggies. Emily's family already had three of our dogs between her mom and her boyfriend and herself - and she had sent countless people our way to adopt from Akron where she lives....A recent conversation about our labs made her visit the website and ask for more pictures of our special needs boy - (who we affectionately called Tri-Pod) - and then she sent me the message that made my heart leap with hope.

"Really?" I asked her - tentatively feeling out her intentions...."Yes - I can't stop thinking about him...." She explained to me how she and her boyfriend had just gotten full custody of his son and they were searching for a dog that would be good with children.....
"Oh - you can't get a better dog than Vader...." I told her....He doesn't even know he is handicapped..."

Our frequent texts about him turned into a date for Emily to come and visit Vader at the rescue....I could tell Emily did not know what to expect from Vader because, he was, afterall - a Tri-Pod....but as I opened up the rescue room door to Vader - once free from his kennel - he leaped in the air and ran around the room to greet his adoption suitor. She laughed with amazement as how agile and wonderful he was...."I was afraid he couldn't walk....I can't believe how he doesn't even know he is missing a leg,"

He pranced around the front room - running over to her to kiss her face and jump in the air to try to hug her...and then he ran around again - as if to show her that he was just like any other baby and worthy of a good home....
"I really want him" Emily said - her eyes shining - so in love with this beautiful boy...."I know that Travis will be crazy for him!"
So I went back to bath up Vader and get him all ready for his new home.
As I bathed Vader - I thought about Emily and what an awesome thing she was doing. Her heart is just so wonderfully big....I knew that she and her boyfriend Ron had gone through a struggle to get custody of his son, and here she was doing everything she could to give Travis a wonderful home with his father...I also thought about what she was doing for Vader - and how his last six weeks had been a struggle to get a new forever home ...and how she was doing everything she could to give him a great home, too. What a completely selfless and wonderful woman she was - and what a good guy her boyfriend Ron was to say yes to her loving plans!! Truly in this home blessings abounded!

Emily left with Vader in her car and with hugs of appreciation and affection from all of us at the rescue.
Each day I get updates from Emily on how Vader is doing and how Travis is doing with Vader.....but I never really worried much because he is in the home of a loving family and in the arms of a loving momma and poppa....
Today I got a picture from Emily...It is of Travis eating cereal – his bowl balance atop the back of Vader – who is sprawled lovingly on Travis' Lap....It speaks volumes more than I ever could about just how happy Vader is in his new home - the place where struggles end and new love begins...a forever place where love grows.....Thank you Emily and Ron for providing Vader such a place. He and Travis are undoubtedly two lucky lucky boys!!

"And after you have suffered a little while, the God of all grace, who has called you to his eternal glory in Christ, will himself restore, confirm, strengthen, and establish you." 1Peter 5:10

"Our Meeka"

She arrived the day that Santa Pictures were being taken at the rescue...December 13, 2014 - A big day for us - an even larger day for her...She had five 4-week old puppies with her...The pups were pretty healthy - aside from a little bit of eye goooo - but the momma we knew only by her name - Meeka - was skin and bones. She was giving all of her nutrients to her babies and she herself needed some TLC and some extra food and nutrients. This is why she had come to us.

She was originally from West Virginia - and because we were so far away and were asked to take her in - (and we said yes, of course) - a three-person transport was arranged and she arrived at the rescue at about 5pm. We truly just had time enough to feed her and place them all in a huge cage in the front of the shop so that they could get to know us before we left for the night.

The next morning - she barked and growled at us if we came too near...Can't blame a good momma for being protective of her pups in a strange and unfamiliar place after a long journey to get here...but in just a few hours - after she had observed us with other doggies and after we'd fed her and cleaned the cage of her little family - she brightened and began kissing our hands and licking our faces.

In the days that followed - Meeka's pups became strong and began eating on their own. They became independent - and she played with them with all of her heart to make them strong and ready for anything. As they grew - she would watch them from the big Orange chair that sits in the front room...We began calling it "Meeka's chair" because it seemed she was always in it. She also became the front door greeter - and our lunch companion - gleaning french fries, pizza crust, and hamburger leftovers from volunteers and family who could not resist her big brown eyes....

She watched her puppies grow up and be adopted...she became housebroken and well trained - learning to sit and shake and lay down....She gained weight and her coat became shiny and beautiful....and we began to realize it was time for her to find a home. Our work with her was done - but our love for her was so huge that we hesitated in actively trying to find her a home because it had to be a great home where she could play - and be loved - and be treated as special as she had always been to us.....

Good dogs deserve great homes - and the call for Meeka's came on Saturday when Sherri called to ask about our large dogs. "It will be my only dog - whichever one I get - but it has to be good with children and kind of trained..." She said. My mind went to all of the really large dogs we had - including the big puppies that had just gotten dropped off at the rescue...."I'll come take a look" Sherri said "I'll know my dog when I see it.." she told me confidently.

Sherri arrived with her adorable niece and nephew and told me "They spend a lot of time with me - so the doggie has to love them, too." I thought this was so wise. I paraded lots of dogs in front of her - and none of them really caught her eye...None of them until Meeka came flying into the front room from the back door where she had been playing in the sun outside....She immediately went to the children while I was trying to corral other dogs who had snuck in the open door, too.

"Ooooh - I like this one..." Sherri said...and I turned around to see that it was Meeka. Meeka had planted herself in front of the family and was doing all of her tricks for them as Sherri's nephew gave commands. "She is a really good dog..."Sherri said..."Why didn't you show me her?" she asked. I laughed and said "I thought you wanted big and I don't think of Meeka as that big..." Sherri laughed "She is big enough...great with the kids...I think she is perfect!"

Sherri asked all kind of questions about Meeka and all of the answers were met with an "Excellent" or "Oh wow! Fantastic!" from Sherri....Meeka kept playing with the kids and Nuzzling Sherri's hand while we talked....It was a no-brainer - Meeka had chosen them.

When the decision was made - and Meeka was bathed up - and news spread that she was getting adopted – Michael and Christine – the very dedicated volunteers who had become Meeka's Family - came of the back where they were scrubbing and feeding. We all had to give ourr goodbyes to Meeka and to meet the wonderful person who she had chosen to take her home.

There they stood - the happy family with Meeka - her nose pressed against Sherri and her tail wagging against the legs of the children. Once she had her collar on and the leash was tightly in Sherri's hands - Meeka was ready for her new adventure....We kissed her and hugged her and cried happy tears as she kissed us back for the last time and waited patiently for her adventure to begin. Sherri and the kids walked through the door and Meeka's nose gloriously followed - and we watched every bit of her leave and jump into their car and go. If you have ever wondered if it is possible to be overwhelmed with joy and at the same time heartbroken - I can tell you it is indeed possible. Our love for our babies does not end when they get to go to their forever homes - and we often find our hearts straddled between our joy for them and the lump in our throats we feel when we remember....

Yesterday evening - as Chris and I cleaned up the final remains of the day and prepared to leave for the night....I said "It seems so weird not to kiss Meeka tonight..." Chris's eyes sparkled and filled up with tears and she said "Yes, I really missed her today...."

We will probably miss her for a long time - but no doubt she is waking up this morning with Sherri, full and happy and loved - on her new journey in her forever home.

"Surely there is a future, and your hope will not be cut off." Proverbs 23:18

"A Big Deal"

Theresa had emailed a few times about the collie-heeler puppy that was left at the rescue....the last one of the litter. She asked many questions and I tried as well as I could to answer them all....She told me that she wanted to send some pictures of the puppy to her husband's phone and that they had to talk about the puppy as a family, and then they would decide. I often hear this from prospective adopters and then never hear from them again...but when I got a text back from her later in the week about the puppy again, she sounded confident and happy to tell me that she would be bringing her husband and her children the next day to see the puppy and possibly adopt her. "The kids don't get out of school until about 3, so it will probably be around 4 if that is ok?" she asked....OF course I said yes...."We are there till 5" I assured her...

The next day was very busy and I found myself running back and forth across the street from the new rescue to the old building several times to greet grooming customers and work on the house. It was late in the day when my husband came into the house and said

"There's a family across the street playing with a puppy...I think they want to see you." Immediately I thought of Theresa.

"Oh...right!" I said and flew across the street again - through the front room of the rescue and out into the side yard. There I found the most adorable family....Two of the prettiest children I had ever seen and a very sweet couple watching these children play. They were running wildly across the yard with the collie-heeler pup jumping at their heels and licking their faces whenever he could get a chance. It was such a sweet little scene I walked up on - I wanted to stand back and watch it all unfold.

Instead, I walked up to Theresa and introduced myself. She smiled and introduced her husband Arturo, and said the kids were having a ball, bonding with the pup. "So how are they doing?" I asked. The little boy heard me and dropped to my side from his full run towards the doggie. "Actually," he said in a very grown up voice, "I think I would like this puppy." I looked at his mom and dad and mouthed "Actually" they laughed "He is very mature." I said. Then I asked him "Do you think you can help take care of him?" And he responded "As long as he is good with children."

I looked at his parents again and gave a huge eye-roll which meant "Too adorable!" They giggled with pride at their very grown-up young man.
The sister, on the other hand - was running around - hair flying in the wind and squealing - the puppy jumping after her and them both falling in the grass and rolling around. Not once did I hear the mom say "you are going to get dirty" Not once did I hear the dad say "Not so loud!!" The parents stood there watching the pure joy of their children with their soon-to-be new puppy and they just beamed.

"We have been thinking about a puppy for a very long time...." Theresa said to me. "It's kind of a big deal."

And when the time came for the little family to decide whether or not they were going to take the puppy home or not - (which I already knew they would) - Theresa and Arturo asked their children if they were ready to make a commitment to the puppy. They both ran up to me and shook their heads "yes" so hard I thought they were going to get whiplash. And as I produced the paper work for the puppy and the adoption agreement...Theresa pulled two very neatly folded "money bags" out of her purse....A twenty, three ones and two dollars in quarters in each little zip-lock baggie.

I looked at her confused as she handed one to each child and then told them "Ok - it's time to pay for your doggie." The kids each handed me a bag and backed away - looking me deeply in the eyes and saying "Thank You."

Finally I understood. I looked at Theresa and gasped "Oh - this is THEIR money?" Theresa nodded "They've saved their money...doing chores, birthday money, just everything." she said. I teared up and looked again at the neatly

folded money in the baggies and realized what her words meant.
"It is a big deal" I said...Wiping my eyes. Theresa and Arturo looked a little
teary, too...."Yes, "Arturo echoed..."It is."

I went into the back room and told my friend and assistant Christine - and
showed her the little money bags that the children had brought and we both
broke down at the cuteness and sweetness of these kids getting one of our
puppies.

And - as the little family walked through the rescue to the front door - we
commended them on being such thoughtful and responsible parents....And they
all stopped at the door to hug us and thank us for rescuing the puppy that would
become their new family member. And as they drove away I felt thankful to
God for the work we do - and that he chose us to do it. At that moment, I think
Chrissy and I both felt a renewed blessing of what we do every day....Because to
us sometimes it's just the work we were given and day in and day out it seems
like nothing really...but on that day we knew to this family...it was a really big
deal.

"The Lord will fulfill his purpose for me; your steadfast love, O Lord,
endures forever. Do not forsake the work of your hands." Psalm 138:8

"Houndie goes to College."

I had no idea what they were looking for when they walked into the rescue - and neither did they....Brice and his mom Jane had found our address on line - had seen some pictures of some doggies and decided to come down from their home in Copley to take a look....They were looking for a dog that Brice could take with him to college - because his housing unit allowed dogs. Brice was going off to finish his senior year and only had a handful of classes to complete his Marketing degree, so he wanted a companion pet with him this year to help him pass the time and to be his buddy at school.

So Jane and Brice walked in and looked around. I told them to let me know who they wanted to meet and they seemed a bit overwhelmed by our selection, Small. Loud. Cute. Young. Old. All of them wiggled in front of Brice and his mom, and they walked around lost in our showroom of puppy and doggie love.

After a bit of "Oh - this one is cute"...and "Look at this one"...they settled in front of the cage of one of the Dalmatian - hound mix females who had spent her entire childhood in our rescue. She had come in with eight of her siblings in a litter and had seen each one get a home amid hundreds (literally) of others - and yet they still waited and watched on standby.... still hoping. Houndie Girl - as we called her - looked up at Brice and literally fell in love with him. He looked down at her in the cage and I think the feeling was mutual.

"I really like this one," Brice said to Jane - and Jane agreed "She has such a pretty face." "Take her out for a walk." I told them - and soon they were slipping a lead over pretty little Houndie Girl's neck and taking her outside.

I watched from the window in horror as Houndie Girl struggled with the lead. None of the Dalmatian mix girls had been walked on a lead much....But instead of walking with Brice and Jane - Houndie Girl wanted to be in Brice's lap and loving on him. She really looked at him with the eyes of love - like I had never seen her do with anyone before. And I think that Brice looked back.

"Oh - this is very good!" I told my husband who was there watching this introduction with me. "This boy really likes her."

As they came inside - Jane had a lot of questions for me that I tried to answer to the best of my knowledge. As a rescue - and not a breeding facility - we do not know everything about our dogs' histories. But I did tell her how Houndie Girl had grown up here and how she had really no permanent name. I told her how she had been waiting and how much I could tell she loved Brice. They spent another while getting to know her inside and outside the rescue...but when the time came for them to make a decision - Jane turned to me and said "I hate to leave her, but our search has just started and we have some other dogs we wanted to visit in other rescues and pounds....But if anyone comes in for her - can you call me first? We really think she is a great dog but want to look around."

I totally understood. And this is where God comes in.

As they left and I put Houndie Girl back in her cage - I said a prayer - giving it up to God. Because as a human - I cannot direct the path of what is to be...I can only hope that it all ends up as God's will. And deep in my heart I knew what I had seen was love....both from this Beautiful Dog and from Brice. I felt that if it was God's will our girl go to college with Brice - God would make it so...

Later that night - my husband asked me "If they wanted to look at more dogs - we have 40 dogs in the rescue....Why didn't you keep showing them dogs?" I smiled because I had seen this same scenario play out at the rescue many times. When a dog finds its way into a human's heart - no other will replace it or better it....I knew that Brice really loved Houndie Girl...and I believed he and his mom needed time to look around at other places just to give them time to see what was out there and make this discovery for themselves. Besides - I had already given it to God and

155

believed in Him for the answer.

And of course - the answer came in the form of question the next morning when I recognized the phone number calling on my phone. "Is she still there???" a frantic Jane asked me on the other end of the line. "I had a horrible dream last night that she ran away and we couldn't get her...." Jane told me. I asked her how the dog hunting went in other places and she laughed...."We looked at all kinds of dogs yesterday - but Brice kept talking about your Girl....and of course no other dog even measured up since we met her first. We should have just stopped looking right then and there....but we are on our way down after we run some errands.....PLEASE don't get rid of her."

I smiled as I hung up the phone and looked up to the heavens with tears running down my face. "God you are so good!" I whispered....

I am not certain that Houndie Girl waited so long so that she could end up with Brice - but I do know that she had certainly waited long enough and if she was going to get a home and be treated with love and cared for like a princess - Brice was the man she was looking for.

As I took Houndie Girl out and placed her in the bathtub to get her all prettied up for her adoption - I told her own story to her as I scrubbed her down and massaged her while I gave her kisses.

"You were such a little girl when you came to us, Houndie..." I told her "And you grew up here and we just love you so much. But today it's your turn to get out of here and start your new life...." I told her as she wiggled and licked my face - returning my kisses....."And oh - by the way..." I told her "Just so you know - you are going off to college.....You are a Marketing major."

".. let us run with endurance the race that is set before us" Hebrews 12:1

"Kindred Spirits"

"I called about the Dalmatian," the lady said as she and her husband came through the door of the rescue. I was not at all prepared for what I saw. On the phone the woman had spoken of her husband - once having a Dalmatian and being very active - but the man I saw with her did not look well enough to be very active at all. I was immediately worried that our "Purdie" - the beautiful female Dalmatian they were coming to see might be too much for him.

I brought her out to greet them, and Purdie - who was always a little shy to begin with - walked right over to the man who'd down sat on a chair waiting to meet her. She came and stood right under the chair - like she belonged there.

"Well this is a good sign" I said to the lady - whose name was Denise. We decided to walk outside so that they could all get better acquainted.

Once outside - the woman's husband - whose name was Fred - walked off with the Dalmatian - down the parking lot towards the garage - petting her the whole time Fred was a bit bent over and his arm just touched the top of Purdie's head - naturally as they walked.

"Is your husband ill?" I asked Denise - who gave me a knowing smile and began to answer me. "He was a POW in Vietnam. Four years and seven months." she said proudly - as if she'd answered questions like mine dozens of times before. "He has PTSD and is all crippled up from Agent Orange...but he does just great." I looked up and saw him walking along with Purdie - her gait matched his as he held the leash and they walked together.

"He was captured two days after his twenty-first birthday - in January of 69 and was released after the French treaties in 1973." She said "I cannot imagine the horrors he went through - but he does talk about it which helps. Not all of the fellas that go to the Vet hospital do - but Fred does" I looked up to watch Fred again and saw him in a whole different light - imagining him as a young soldier and what he once must have been, and done, and seen.

I also thought about my own brother-in-law, Wayne, who I never met - who was killed in the same country where Fred did all that time as a captive. I thought about the pictures that hang on the walls of the place I now call home of Wayne as a young man - and how Fred was also just no more than a kid when he was a captive in the same war. It made me see Fred and Purdie as - really - a boy and his dog.....and my eyes filled with tears....Denise must have read my thoughts and my face - because she said "Fred and a dog - well - that's really the best thing for him."

I watched as Fred stopped to regain his balance - just as Purdie walked between his legs and looked straight up at him - as if to steady him. This brought me to full tears - not just tears running down my face - but I stood there blubbering like a child - full sob - and I excused myself for a tissue. As I walked in the rescue - Fred walked back towards Denise and by the time I'd blown my nose and gotten myself together - they were telling me that Purdie was definitely going home with them. I told them I'd bathe her up and get her all pretty for her new life.....

And as I stood with the warm water running on Purdie and tears still streaming down my face - I thought what an appropriate match this was going to be....because we really didn't know all that much about Purdie -

what she had been through and what she had put up with. She acted as though she may have lived through her own captivity and feelings of being lost several times in her life - just like Fred. And from the moment she'd met him - she seemed to sense a sameness of spirit - a kindred need. I whispered to her as I rinsed her and patted her dry "You will be just right for each other. I am so happy for you!"

As I came back out to the front room of the rescue - Fred was sitting and waiting for her - and she walked up and nuzzled her head under his hand and looked up at him.
"HIS dog!" Denise laughed - and they prepared to go.

I gave both Denise and Fred a hug and a kiss on the cheek.

Thank you so much for everything you did for us." I said to Fred and I looked closely at this Vietnam hat and all the medals he had on it ...My eyes rested on the pin that said "POW" and I immediately got tears again. "Oh - you're welcome!" he said cheerfully and unassumingly - like it really wasn't anything - and he gave my arm a squeeze. "Come on girl." he said to Purdie - and I watched him walk out with his hand resting on her head as they walked towards the door. The former soldier - crippled up by his service and the rescue dog with the sketchy past - but truly, a boy and his dog.

"By this all people will know that you are my disciples, if you have love for one another." John 13:35

This evening was born with shades of baby blue and pink.....the beginning of night hung between the end of daylight and the falling of darkness..... and it wrapped the sky with nursery room hues as the coolness of dusk's first breaths washed over me as I drove home....Another successful adoption....another wonderful day....both behind me and yet I could only see the night ahead as another beginning.....

For in this life - the life of rescue - there is no end in sight....Only time that has passed and time that waits for the next opportunity to make a difference - to go where God would have me go...and to change the life of a helpless and voiceless baby.....be it 8 weeks, 8 months or 18 years.....

I see the night as the beginning of their slumber, a reprieve from the truth they live knowing that they are homeless ....and waiting....Not the end of the day - but the start of their nightly dreams of a home...of slippers on their backs and a big thick rug upon which to nap....of children laying their sleepy heads upon them and warm parents to lie with after all is quiet in the house.

And as I shut off the lights at the shelter and walk out into the baby blues and pretty pinks of the evening - I whisper a prayer to the Heavens to keep them all safe, find them all homes, and let tomorrow be another opportunity to make their dreams come true....And from this nursery room sky - be born many happy beginnings.

51902383R00089

Made in the USA
Charleston, SC
06 February 2016